By The Light of a Two Faced Moon

by Jessica Reynolds

By the Light of a Two Faced Moon

Published by Blood Quill Press
ISBN: # 979-8-218-72112-1
1st Printed Edition October 6th, 2025

"Someone I loved once gave me a box full of darkness.
It took me years to understand that this too, was a gift."
~ Mary Oliver

Thank you everyone who has ever given me a box full of darkness, and to the kindred souls who have loved me despite my own.

✧   **Mom:** Thank you for always believing in me. You are the reason why I fell in love with words. (P.S. That thesaurus really came in handy.)

✧   **Sissy:** I love you more than my luggage. You are my person, and the only reason I stayed.

✧   **Chris:** You are the greatest love of all of my lives. The stories we have told together are everything.

✧   **Cassidy:** Everything with you was magic. I will cherish our memories forever and always.

Letter to my Readers

Hello,

I usually skip introductions such as these because I'm often too eager to read on. However, if you'll stay with me for a moment, I would like to share a few important things before you begin.

This book was written over the span of my years and with that comes the good, the bad, and the ugly. Living with a neurodivergent mind and an empathetic heart, I've experienced life deeply, sometimes painfully so.

Within these pages you'll find poems that touch on sensitive subjects including: death, domestic abuse, eating disorders, erotica, grief, mental illness, miscarriage, self-harm, sexual assault, suicidal thoughts, and violence. Don't worry, every chapter will note if these subjects are present, so you can decide if you would like to explore that section.

My poetry collection is also grouped by theme and organized alphabetically. After many attempts to shape them into a flowing narrative, I realized they are just as random and scattered as I am.

If you choose to read my story, my hope is that if any of the darker poems resonate with your own struggles, you'll find the help, support and love that I eventually did. You do not have to battle your demons alone, even if the voice inside your head tries to convince you otherwise.

Medicine and therapy saved my life, and they may save yours too. There is always hope, friend. Not for a perfect life, but for a better one. Really, a perfect life would be far too boring anyway.

Thank you, dear reader, for letting me share these pieces of myself with you.

All my love,
Jessica

Table of Contents

✧ Prologue

✧ Anxiety

✧ Depression

✧ Kinship

✧ Lovesick

✧ Heartbreak

✧ Divine

✧ Violation

✧ Suicide

✧ Healing

✧ Epilogue

Anxiety

. the voice that trembles .
[Eating Disorders, Self-harm]

A-Mused

Typing, typing.
I'm typing these words,
asking my muse to come forth.
She is needed to translate this story
from my mind onto this digital paper,
but she is too wired on caffeine
cleaning out the space between my ears.
There is dust swirling out of my sinuses
but it does not stir a thought.
Not one,
not one from me.

Writing, writing.
These awkward words keep forming.
Imploring my muse to come forth.
She is needed to organize this mess of plot
from my mind onto this paper.
But she is swerving and swaying
trying to control this train of thought,
and the tracks aren't leading anywhere.
Nowhere,
nowhere for me.

Humming, humming.
I am humming to keep from screaming.
Begging my muse to come forth.
Oh, how she is needed to compose this book
from my mind onto this paper,
but she is laughing and wrestling
holding my tongue in cheek.
Letting my voice say nothing.
No thing,
nothing but jumbled speak.

And, Scene

I pretended I got the news today,
and on cue my thoughts reel to life
as a spotlight illuminates the stage
to envision my greatest fear:
Hypochondriac Edition 2.0.
Suddenly a clapperboard snaps
loudly shut in my mind.
    "More drama! More passion!"
my inner credit demands,
    "Action!"
So, I initiate the iteration
of this most tragic of scenes,
until I have fine tuned
the nuances to near perfection.

Sitting next to me,
manic eyes glued to the screen,
is the tortured muse
of my obsessive thoughts.
Anxiety is wringing her nervous hands
as if they were a perpetually too moist rag.
She whispers softly,
    "What if it is even worse than that?"
My heart squeezes tight
like a sanguine stress ball
aching to burst within my chest.
I feel my leg starting to bounce,
like a nervous rabbit thumping
in panicked morse code.

Yes, we all know the rules
of the infamous Game.
As soon as you think of it
-you lose.
It is Anxiety's favorite ploy
to invite me down

the doomscroll rabbit hole
of my morbid thoughts.
21 questions is for chumps.
Instead, we like to play:
999 paranoid and oddly specific,
(but somehow definitely possible)
demoralizing scenarios for the soul.

However, before we can commence,
my therapist pushes the wide brim
of her spectacles up her nose.
(This signals what she is about to say
is a key breakthrough in the plot.)
    "Anxiety might seem like your nemesis,
    but in actuality she is your protector."
My inner credit rolls her eyes and boos.
Nevertheless, she continues,
    "She wants you to feel safe,
    and that is done out of love...not hate."
The laugh track ensues inside of my head.
    "Thanks," I say. "I'm cured."

Broken Record

Am I repeating myself?
I keep on writing the same tired words,
the same clichéd metaphors.
I am a broken record skipping,
saying the same thing over and over-
  saying the same thing over and over-
    saying the same thing...

Even I grow weary of this overplayed tune.
I desperately want to write something new.
Still my mind is obsessed,
humming this sullen theme song.
Can a soul fall in love with sadness?
If I stepped out of melancholy's dresses
would I even recognize my reflection?

Sometimes healing feels like betrayal,
like make-believe.
Reciting the lines that everyone wants to hear
until even you begin to agree
the encouraging lie,
the comforting lie,
the promising lie.

When you have a lifetime's worth
of acting experience
you are so very good at fooling everyone,
even yourself.
Am I fooling myself?
How can I ever know if this is working
when I'm so very good at pretending?

Chantey

I carry the ocean inside of
this shipwrecked heart.
It rocks against my ribs,
never serene.
In the midst of
the swelling surf,
so turbulent and troubled,
I carve cries for help
in the sand of my skin.
Trying to let this storm
thunder its tantrum
over the vast
and restless waves.
And I?
I am a careless sailor,
chasing the teasing tide
to anywhere but here.
My pleas drowned out
by the roar of the salty sea.

Eat Me

I'm teetering on the edge
of should or shouldn't.
Rocking on that razor edge
of panicked indecision.
One moment before I'm reaching,
gulping down the blue pill
of make-believe and comforting lies.
Promising myself that next time
I'll make the right choice.
Yes, the next time I'll choose red.

There is always a next time,
but there is never another choice.
It's always the same hand I feed from,
starving for momentary satisfaction.
Stodgy mornings after.
Full of belly, head and heart aches.
You told me,
    "You can be anything you want to be.
    All you have to do is believe."
Why would you lie to me?

My greatest folly:
surmising that the last time
wasn't the last time after all.

Funambulism

It starts
with the slap of frustration
and my breath tightens in my chest,
a slithering constrictor coiling
around my lungs
that forces the air out
in a tight, harsh sigh.

    "Are you alright?"
The sound alarms.
Suddenly, a spotlight shines
too brightly in my eyes.
    "I am fine."

I pull my smile taunt across my lips,
a tightrope of lies.
And I, a practiced performer,
know how to carefully tread
across the tension in our conversation.
How to balance so perfectly
in the sway of your concern
that you learn to look away.

But behind this bony prison
of clinched white teeth
lies a graveyard of haunted words.
Pinned by the tentacle of my tongue
and slain by the silence of this choking air.

    I am not ok.
I am a terrified child
cowered in the corner of my mind
chanting the words to a prayer,
    "I am fine, I am fine, I am fine."
Hoping to convince
even me, myself and I.

The Game

My mouth an open wound,
apologies like Band-Aids
over my sorry lips.
Ripped off and pushed down
so often they never stick.

My anxious tongue
licking the tension from my teeth.
Always wanting to say the right thing.
Nevertheless, I say the wrong thing.

Unable to win this made-up game,
an abacus clicking,
tallying up my misspoken words.
My mind a dutiful scoreboard
flashing with each flustered syllable.

Your awkward laughter
follows a pat of your hand,
    "You don't need to say you're sorry."
So I apologize for apologizing.

You don't understand the rules,
or how desperately I need to win
this game my brain has rigged.

Gilded Cage

She had poems perched
on the lip of her mouth,
but they trembled
like a nervous flutter of wings.

Vulnerable, reluctant,
afraid to speak out.
Every word swallowed.

She, full of sentences.
Her throat salty
from chasing them with tears.

No songs are sung
from this self-made cage.

Only belly aches
from torn out pages.
Her story a delicacy,
only she's tasted.

Good Enough

She strained against the steadfast bolt
as it angrily bit down on the metal.
Rusted, stubborn
melded on by its dying will.
It would not budge.

The wrench left imprints
into her red palms.
Her teeth locked in place,
her lungs burned as
tiny veins raised on her skin
like blue rivers of resolve.

Finally, her breath released in a half sob.
Her shoulders slumped
as her sweaty back slid down
the pebbled wall in defeat.

Head in hands,
she remembered the first time
she was told that a girl:
will never be as strong as a boy,
will never be as useful as a boy,
will never be as worthy as a boy.

It was the first time her body
had ever failed her.
She had never doubted
herself until now.

Her confidence unwound
like a key-turned doll, settled.
Only good enough now
for dances, dresses,
and tea parties.

Manic

It happens in a moment
and my smile lights up the room.
I can't help but feel my body
swaying to the music.
It's loud and so upbeat
I feel my body buzzing,
and my brain feels absolutely
ecstatic, energetic, euphoric.
I just want to move,
and suddenly
I can do anything!
My mind is racing,
my heart is pacing,
and I just want to scream!
I'm so fucking happy,
and it has been so long
since I just felt happy.
It feels like I'm high–
no, no, no,
this feels like my normal.
Because when you are stuck
on an up-and-down roller coaster
then it's either high or low baby.
In a flash the sad sea is gone,
and I'm not drowning anymore.
Yes, I'm flying!
Just like Wonder Woman,
I'm untouchable up here
in my invisible jet.
It's as if the pilot switched life
from slow-mo to fast forward.
Everything is accelerating
at the speed of light,
and I laugh...
and goddamn
the sound of my laughter

sounds like the sweetest thing.
It's pouring out of me,
and I finally feel alive again.
So, I leave this bedroom tomb behind,
because I've been resurrected.

Night Raider

Quiet bickering of the wind
hushing through the trees.
Arguing with the screen door
who refuses to shut.
An otherwise eventless night.
A star-gone moonless night.
Full of tension,
promising a lightning show.
The clouds growl over the town.
And even I, in a warm snug bed
shiver in blanket clothes.
Sleep refuses to take me,
as the skyborne tears
slice through the waiting dark.
The thunder's growl a sign
the worst has come.
So, I quiet my fears,
and hope the storm
doesn't have me in its eye.

Pretty

All the pretty horses
lined up in a row,
lined up like the pretty idols
paper collaged on your bedroom walls.
Denial inside
this Pretty, Pretty Princess game.
Face paint all your makeup.
Less is more,
it gives you character.
Pretty music playing,
do you care to dance?
Two step,
  three step,
    four step,
      twirl.
And is it easy?
Oh so easy,
to be so perfectly easy
to impress?
So you dress
for the occasion,
for the evasion
of your therapy.
You're not pretty,
you're not free,
and all the faces in the magazine
will never let you live it down.

The Ritual

I try to wash my hands of this.

I scrub and scrub and scrub,
but they never feel
quite clean enough.

Something twitches,
like microscopic worms
under my skin,
feasting on the festering.

My palms blush
as the blood boils
under the scald
of soap and sanitizer.

Then I pat them dry,
hopeful, but the stain
has already started seeping
to the surface again.

I baptize them
in bleach and bubbles,
and pray to feel holy again.

They are too raw to touch
with the soft towel.
So, I let them drip
into the sink this time.

I know this is senseless.
I know what rots
lies just beneath the surface.

Wild and untamed, growling
in the hollow of my guts.

Pounding a tortured plea
in the drum of my ears.

Rattling my achy bones,
in this stuffy meat suit closet.

It is the bad thing I buried long ago,
that consumes me from the inside.

The only way to truly kill it–
with kindness, acceptance, forgiveness.
I cannot absolve myself of this.
So, I sigh and start anew.

I try to wash my hands...

Siesta Barista

The last drop of the coffee drip
in my mouth is bitter,
and leaves with it a coarse grind.
Like an oyster I try to tongue it.
Round and round,
a tiny pebble of annoyance,
A black pearl?
No, just a rough bit
of burnt residue,
that begs the question,
    "Should I have one more cup or two?"
Anything to keep me awake.

    Sigh.

I happen to know
after thirty-six hours of not sleeping
you're dreaming.
Nevertheless, I don't want to crawl
back into my bed defeated,
to battle my thoughts in darkness.
Too long have I distracted my mind,
terrified of its silence.

The world shifts like a kaleidoscope
as I blink my eyes in slow motion.
Taking tiny naps when they're not open.

Damnit!
Why do I have to sleep?
I've done nothing...
nothing but patron a hard-working Columbian,
and write poems to keep from dozing.

Voices

It's just my anxiety speaking,
I hear myself think again today.
And the realization dawns on me
that this nervous part of me
has been given a voice,
while I have stood there
a mute girl
with apologies for hands.
Hiding eyes that are oceans,
salty and on the verge of tears.
My breath comes in waves,
legs trembling,
as if I'm sinking
into quicksand.
Like a clumsy ballerina,
I stumbled outside the store
gulping for air.
Tired of drowning on dry land.
In a sea of crowds,
I'm a frantic bird
scanning the horizon
for some safe harbor.
When you grab my hand
with asking eyes,
and my body tenses as if to scream.
But then all I hear is my voice
lying, saying,
    "I'm fine dear."

Yes Girl

Yes Girl lip's beam a smile,
too prematurely,
as you start to ask her
anything.
Her eyebrows perked
at the trigger words.
She so desperately wants
to please.

Yes Girl nods her head,
too eagerly,
already agreeing to do
anything.
Her voice cheerily
reassuring you
she's really saved the date
this time.

Yes Girl starts to pace,
too anxiously,
as she tries to think of
anything.
Some plausible excuse
believable enough,
so you won't hate her
for canceling.

Yes Girl chews her nails,
as the deadline inches closer...

Yes Girl's blood pressure rises
as you text, "Hey are you coming?"

Yes Girl wants to throw up,
but instead types out an apology.

Yes Girl crawls into bed,
too exhausted,
from even trying
anything.
    "Are you mad at me?" she asks.
    You message back, "Of course not."
Bless your heart
for lying.

Depression

. a black hole where a soul should live .
[Depression, Self-harm]

After the Beep

It's getting bad again.
I can tell by the way
my bed summons me
to its blanket embrace
over and over again.

I've silenced my phone,
stopped checking
my calendar alerts.

I don't want to know
what day this is.
It is better to be
blissfully ignorant,
or so they say.

Or else my brain will start
calculating how many
days have passed since
that appointment,
   that due date,
     that deadline.

I'll hide undercover
in the fog of war instead.
Where everyone is sleeping,
and no one can find me
in my homemade quarantine.

Procrastinating until
it's far too late
to fix anything.

You try to call me back
to the real world.
I'm so sorry friend

I just forgot to switch off
Do Not Disturb mode again.
These excuses sounding off
like an answering machine.

Band-Aid Clinic

Emergency room visit, three am.
Empty chairs with open arms.
I am too busy pacing
to relax in their embrace.
Unread magazine covers
scattered around the waiting zone,
and a TV that entertains
no one listening in the room.
Beeping signals, whispering tongues,
hush-hushed for the doctor's call.
So I am left on stand-by,
favoring my cigarette over the Lysol.

Bitter Pills

She takes the pills,
tiny gravel on her tongue.
They chalk in her mouth
and grumble down her throat.
She chugs the stale
nightstand water,
and grinds her teeth
at the aftertaste.
She shoves open
the rusty storm door
and lumbers out into the sun
still in last week's
unwashed clothes.

She did all the things
she was supposed to do,
and yet she is not better.

She did all the things
she was supposed to do,
and yet she is still tired.

So, she flings her body
onto her unmade bed
like it was something
she did not want to wear.
Tossed and turned until her linens
entrapped her in
a blanket cocoon.
She stayed buried
all the spring,
and yet she did not bloom.
So, she shushed her mind
and begged for sleep
but instead lay awake
marinating in the gloom.

She did all the things
they said for her to do,
and yet she is not better.

She did all the things
they said for her to do,
and still she is so tired.

They say it gets better.
They say it takes time.
So, she believes the lies
and chokes on tears
she'd rather cry.
It's so much better
than the ugly truth,
a much more bitter pill
than antidepressants.

Cursed

I have always had a tilted tongue.
Half-drunk on poetry,
half-starved for love.
Like dangling carrots
my stubborn ass
made earrings out of food.
Always struggling to enjoy
something I already have.

I weep to the universe
crying out in hungry honks
for being cursed in this form.
My guides shake their heads,
and attempt to gently
unclasp my jewelry.
I kick out with wild eyes,
fearful they have robbed me.
They try to comfort me,
but their hands look like weapons,
unfamiliar and controlling.
So I speed away panting.

Now, off the beaten path
a puddle shimmers in the muddy road.
Stretching my short neck to drink it
my stiff knees keep me from reaching.
Woeful eyes flood with tears
that rain down
making the tiny lake grow.
Finally it touches my lips,
and it is too salty.
Oh everything seems like curses
when you are grateful for nothing.

Dark Eyed Girl

Dark-eyed girl
seen too much of the world
has a heart too soft,
and a mind too heavy.
Take in what you can,
leave what you can't carry.
For your heart is too big
and your mind is too weary.

Dark-eyed girl
wants to save the world
but has a heart too bruised,
and a mind too messy.
Save yourself,
let go of what you can't carry.
Because your heart is an anchor
and your mind is a ferry.

Dark-eyed girl
runs away from the world
has a heart too glum,
and a mind too leery.
Find your peace,
release what you can't carry.
So your heart can heal
and your mind can tarry.

Envy

In truth,
I crave honesty,
because I rarely
disclose it to myself.

As if I could not be trusted
with its bluntness.
The battering ram of revelation
bruising my too tender ego.

Or contrarily, it's sharpness.
The raw edge of reality
slicing across my tender heart
like a paper-thin cut.

I'd be lying If I told you it didn't hurt.

Perhaps the masochist in me,
craves the brutality of integrity.
While the sadist in me,
delights to watch me cry.

Flake

I've been avoiding you because
I cannot come out
of this shell of a home.
I know your softest hope
will be gutted once again
when I tell you no.
I know you think I'm a flake:
undependable and
unfathomably absent.
But I'm really just scared
that if I saw you again
you'd see me
and how beastly I've been.

Hush

You open your mouth to speak,
but only silence comes out.
Words stuck to your teeth
like sweet, sticky taffy,
but I hear you.
Sometimes silence
is louder than sentences.

Is Just

My heart is just an empty cup,
dipped in a thirsty sea.
Not a single tear dares to shed
from the midnight void in me.

My mind is just a broken clock
wound too tight, ticking endlessly.
Not a single sound from it chimes
a happy melody.

My soul is just a dying star,
a once bright light flickering.
Not a single shimmer was left behind
when the darkness swallowed me.

I Realize

Have I ever loved myself?
I say those three familiar words.
Offer them up to the mirror,
but I cannot accept them
as it feels disingenuous,
this soliloquy.

Am I supposed to make-believe
that I truly deserve
admiration for mediocrity?
Praise for the bare minimum?
Applause for simply existing
as an unplanned accident?

Do I even know how to love?
I rummage through my memories.
Every atom of warmth gifted to me
I handed back awkwardly.
A mimicked embrace and upturned lips,
so you'd believe it came from me.

Medicine

Some pills make
the ocean of emotion
soothe its tidal waves.

Some pills make
the fog of my brain
clear in the morning light.

Some pills even
quiet the voices,
and unveil the illusions.

But then melancholy,
soft and apathetic,
lingers in my heart.

With the waters calm,
and my head quiet and serene,
depression stays and holds my hand.

Mourning

i.

The clippers buzz to life.
My hand squeezes it tight,
but for once I don't want to do this.
I don't want to shave my head again.
Still, my hand lifts the vibrating machine
to my temple, and I begin to shed
every strand I've tried to grow.
Every thin, wispy curl clinging to my scalp.
I watch the hair collect into the basin,
barely a handful of pepper grey locks.
Such a simple thing, that made me feel
so beautiful once upon a time.
I have heard stories told
of those who cut their hair to grieve.
I guess I am in mourning too.
For the girl I once was,
and the life she could have had.
I stand at the edge of the waste bin,
its darkness a tomb,
and quietly bury the dream of her.

ii.

"Hang in there," she says.
There is kindness in her eyes.
For once I am speechless.
How it must hurt her to see my broken spirit.
   She assumes it is cancer, I think.
I don't have the heart to tell her it's not.
The bell chimes a goodbye as they exit.
Their silhouettes float like happy ghosts
as they pass by the shop window.
I see her husband hug her a little tighter,
as if he suddenly remembered that we are all dying.
Some, a little faster than others.

Ode to Depression

I open the dryer
to dump the clean clothes
into the hamper again.
It's easier than folding them
or tossing them on an unmade bed
only to kick them onto the floor later.
I shuffle into the kitchen,
and stare at the mountain of dishes.
I promise myself I'll do them later.
It is a lie, but I pretend to believe it.
I open the cabinets and fridge
but nothing looks appetizing.
There is nothing nutritional here.
Even so, I tear open the cheap noodles
and dunk them in the water.
This body desperate for substance,
but unable to provide it.
I sink into a creaky chair,
and stare at the screen
yearning for excitement.
I keep doomscrolling,
desperate for distraction.
Nevertheless,
every thing feels the same;
a parody of a happy life
that I'll never know.
So, I tumble back into bed
and write odes to depression.
Too tired to sleep,
but too tired not to.

Series of Distractions

Life has to be more
than a series of distractions.
In the madness of deception
you can never sharpen your perception.
You just keep surpassing signs,
and ignoring the pleas of reason
to stop and listen
to the quiet whisper of the heart.
That seems little more than
a dream memory quickly fading
in the stark bright light of waking.
The head often tries too hard
to pick apart the puzzle
of the mystery
until the pieces lay scattered,
and nothing makes sense or scenery.
Most everything I've learned
has been little more than
desperate coping mechanisms.
A spiral, always a circle,
around old haunts and habits.
And these days I feel
more and more like a ghost,
hollow and placeless,
passing through,
passing through
a series of distractions.

Spoons

I grasp these silver spoons,
so tarnished and so few,
and try not to glance
at others' heaping drawers
full of so much more.
My mind yearns to achieve
an overflowing list of things.
However, it takes two
just to get out of bed,
and another to cry in the shower.
How quickly they dwindle down
til my empty hands
help me crawl back into bed.
Less is more they say,
but those privileged few
have never truly hungered,
having been spoon-fed
all of their dreams.
This is the hand you're dealt.
    Be grateful! I tell myself.
So, I take my spoonful of medicine,
because I can't afford the sugar
to make this bitter sweeter.

Surviving

Surviving, not living.
Day in, day out.

Sun dawns and sets
then fades to black.

Heart pulsing, heat cooling,
breath stutters unsteady.

Smokey and laced,
cigarette taste.

Wine drunk and hungry,
tongue desert thirsty.

Unwashed covers,
ruins of a body.

Haunted and restless,
tremors of sadness.

Conscious...but barely
not living, surviving.

Then Darkness

The air has turned sour,
bitter then tasteless.
A great building storm
has darkened all things.

Yet, there is no terrible thunder,
nor furious lightning,
or even tears to fall like rain.
Everything fades to black.

Like an ill-fated omen,
your impending doom lingers.
It is a slow and quiet death.

Harder to breathe,
harder to dress yourself,
harder to clean anything.

In your procrastination,
the dust has settled like a veil
over your desk so cluttered
it's become a fortress of failure.

This room has become a coffin,
this bed has become a coffin,
this body has become a coffin.

Everyone sees you are stiff and broken.
They circle around like vultures
hungry to mourn you.
You rest, but not in peace.

Sleep laps at your mind
like water upon a shifting shore,
beckoning at your feet like an impish siren
oh so eager to swallow you.

Your eyes droop heavy, sullen and dry.
Your heart beats languidly,
your sigh hushed like a whisper...
then darkness.

Thousand Yard Stare

I wish you could live
in the perdition of my mind
for one goddamn day.

You would crumble to your knees, sobbing
if you knew how much pain I was in.

Nothing is ever easy or free.
I have to fight myself
for every single thing.

How long could your pride
hold its head high
roasted by the gallery
of my peevish critics?

How many times would your pleas
fall on the deaf ears
of my preceding judge?

How long would you stay
bellowing out prayers
in an empty, echoing church?

How many times
would you shadow box
the tormented memories
of my relentless ghosts?

How long could you fake a smile
as my faithful nemesis
gut punches your insides?

How many times could you
defuse the vessel of a soul
that was in self-destruct mode?

I have been at war with myself
for so damn long
that I have lost hope for peacetime.

You shake your head and say,
    "It's all in your head."

But that is where I have
battled every demon
and somehow survived.

And take it from me,
even one minute in hell
feels like a lifetime.

Translation

Claro que si,
mi primer poema
en español está triste.
A pesar de que
me enseñé a mí mismo
nuevas palabras para decir,
todavía no entiendo
cómo traducir
felicidad.

(Of course,
my first poem
in Spanish is sad.
Even though
I taught myself
new words to say,
I still don't understand
how to translate
happiness.)

Unsaid

(A blank page for my thoughts,
for somethings are better left unsaid.)

Ventilation

You crack open the window,
small and cloudy,
above the kitchen sink
and you feel the press
of fresh air on your skin.

Then you realize,
that all you have tasted
for days on end,
has been recycled sighs.

Self-isolation,
before the contagion,
before you had the chance
to ruin everything.

One step back,
you're a little distant.

Two steps back,
salt on your pillow.

Three steps back,
messages on read.

Endless steps back:
starvation.

Fasting from love
so you won't miss it
when it's gone.

Fasting from life
so they won't miss you
when you're gone.

Still, what has depression been, but a lie?
You are already gone.

You have emptied yourself
from every photo album
until you are haunting
nothing but your fantasies.

Nevertheless, this windy kiss
has awakened something.
Your eyes slowly opening
as if from dreaming.

A sadness releasing slowly,
tongued out like a sigh.

You Are

You are a silent whistle
howling in the wind,
no one hears you crying wolf.

You are a pricking needle
pushed into flawless fabric,
all tangled thread and apologies.

You are a too full cup
of southern iced tea,
sickly sweet with sour lemon.

You are a tired trek
through a dune filled desert,
all mirage and no oasis.

Kinship

. lost and found family .
[Domestic Abuse, Grief]

Bambi

I cried today
when I read about fawning.
I pictured myself back then,
a tiny deer collapsed on her belly,
the soft carpet a bed of grass
underneath my terrified heart.

My mother a stoic doe
barking at me to go to my room,
but beneath the shadow
of her angry command
was a secret, desperate plea.
    "Danger! Danger! Hide!"

She would pace the living room
making herself the only target
for the man-shaped predator
she had been a fool to marry.
I hunkered down in the doorway
obedient, but trembling
my tiny body unable to defend you.

I learned today,
that you taught me how to survive
the cruel reality of violent appetites.
To tip-toe through relationships
ever vigilant for the signs of peril.
To soothe the angry growls of lovers
who raised their voices when displeased,
their fists hungry for the soft flesh
of your broken body.

You hid your bruises,
dried your tears,
spit blood into the sink,
brushed your teeth,

and tucked me into bed.

I know you tried to protect me,
but I'm so very tired mother
of witnessing this slaughter.
I wish you would have taught me
to run away instead.

The Chosen

All I ever wanted
was to be loved.
To be someone's favorite.
To be so adored
I could never doubt if
your affection was customary.

My niece told her teacher,
I am the best hugger.
She confides in me,
my scent makes her feel safe.
It is the best compliment
I have ever received.

She is older now.
Gives me a quick squeeze
and hurries out the door.
I have lost my magic.
I want to apologize.
Instead, I only smile
and wave goodbye.

My husband hovers
near my desk edge,
as I have requested.
I have pleaded for a hug
before we say goodnight.
It is the only time
we touch anymore.

I am starved for love,
but this nightly ritual of ours
has inevitably lost its magic.
It is not real love
if you have to beg.

I shuffle off to bed, mine
across the room from his.
It feels as if we are boarding
two separate vessels
to sail away into the night.
He does not ask me to join him.

So, instead I wrap myself
in warm, heavy blankets.
Snuggle an old, stuffed bear
as mangy as I am.
Cry softly into my pillow
as I drift off to sleep.

My mind wanders back,
to my school yard days.
Standing nervously in line.
Listening as the children
call name after name
to fill up their team.

Desperately hoping
someone,
anyone...
would choose me.

Daddy

You, my father, still a stranger.
Nervous fingers dial your number.
A jittery ringing echos in my ear.

"Hello?" you inquire
through the receiver.
A timid silence answers you.

Why can't I speak?
I know it's you!
Why can't I tell you,
I exist?

Dark Room

Mother,
everyday you fade
like a photograph
developed in a dark room,
and never framed properly.

Oh pretty soon you'll be
just another scrapbook memory,
and I am somehow not prepared
to face reality without you here.

Dear Djinn

My eyes are fading
with the color of my jeans.
It's been a long time since
I have asked the clouds for rain,
but when it comes, it pours.

Oh autumn,
with all your pretty dresses
of deep reds and browns.
Your leaves falling down,
leaving you naked and shivering
in the eve of winter.
Sometimes I wish I could shed
every single thing about me,
and blossom new in the spring.

But instead,
I shuffle home from school.
Stepfather is drunk again.
The TV is talking
to no one in the gloom.
So I sigh,
stomp up to my room,
and remember
that wishes only come true
in fairytales, not nightmares.

Doll Face

You say you want to see
my authentic self,
but I don't believe you.
Because most days
I wake up and don the mask.

Some days it's harder
with no caffeinated blood
or too many quick
right-out-of-bed-to-dos.
I don't have time to practice
these rehearsed lines,
or paint on the fake smile
everyone is so content with.

I'm too distracted or tired
but everyone notices.
You think I'm sad,
   you think I'm tired,
      you think I'm sick,
and you are right.

So today I reveal the real me.
The no-makeup me,
the no-dress-up me,
the no-fabricated me...
and you hate it.

You keep frowning, pouting,
asking what could be so wrong.
Ergo I have to pat your hand,
and reassure you it's not your fault.
(It's not, you know.
It is just exhausting
to have to keep saying that.)

Now, not only do I have to
shoulder my depression
I have to tiptoe around your feelings too.
These days it's much more difficult
to put on this performance.
It's harder to convince anyone that I'm alright,
when I don't really believe that myself.

Just for one day I wish
someone would look at me
and mean it when they say,
        "It's ok that you don't feel ok.
        You don't have to hide today."
So, I could finally set this doll face down and
b r e a t h e.

Enemies Closer

At times I wonder
if you were really
my best friend at all.

If you crossed your fingers
with all the promises we made,
and like a child only played along
because you were lonely.

I wonder if you rolled your eyes
every time that I'd call,
and only pretended to be happy.

Did you dread each morning
we'd walk to school,
each girl talk that broke
the silence between us?

And when we'd check out boys
was your giggling only because
you knew you were the prettier one?

How often I'd wonder
if you secretly hated me,
and only kept your enemies closer.

First Born

I hold you tight,
little miracle.
Rainbow baby,
face of my sister,
made in her belly.
You are so perfect.

Oh, how my arms
have ached for this.
I hum to you,
and rock you softly
close to my heart.
I am not a mother,
but I will adore you
just the same.

Every atom in me
alights at your half smiles,
and sleepy eyes.
You carry within you
a tiny piece
of my own mother
who cannot be here
to embrace you,
even though it was
her cherished wish.

My womb
is a barren field
where nothing grows,
but here now
as I feel you grasp my finger
with your tiny hand,
I vow to give you
all my love and hers.

Growing Pains

One day your sweet, sticky fingers
will grow into clean slender ones,
no longer fond of messy memories.

Your infectious smile and giggling hugs
will convert to soft quick squeezes,
and a nod as you rush our goodbyes.

You won't vye for my attention
every waking moment.
Your once wonder filled eyes,
now bored with the world.

I won't over celebrate
every new thing you accomplish
with too-eager praise.
You'll be more experienced now,
and yearn for genuine feedback.

You'll need me less and less each day,
and come to resent my rules
that are only meant to protect you.

Our cuddles will come less frequently
and I'll savor your attention more,
because your independence
will forge a space around you.

I feel such pride and solace
as you begin to spread your wings,
so eager to fly from
this nest I built with love.

March 24th

Today is your birthday, Mom.

I sang you a song.
I brought you flowers.
I even thought to buy you
a tiny slice of cake,
but for the life of me
I could not remember
what flavor was your favorite.

It's been fifteen years since you left,
and I still cannot forgive myself
for not being there with you
when you passed from this world.

You died long before
your youngest daughter
grew into a woman.
I know you wanted to live
to see her graduate school.
I know you knitted a blanket
to give to my first born,
but nothing turned out
the way that we wanted it to.

Sissy has gifted you
five grandchildren.
I see in them pieces of you,
even though they have never
seen your smiling face,
heard your laughter or stories,
nor been swept into
your loving embrace.
She is a good mother, like you.
I know you are so proud of her.

I miss you so very much.
I hope wherever you are
you found heaven,
and was finally able to see
your own mother
waiting there for you
with an open heart and arms.

After a lifetime
of sickness and sorrow,
you deserve love and peace.
It was the thing you asked for
when you blew out
your birthday candles
time and time again.
And I pray the universe
was kind enough
to grant that wish
for you.

Mother Knows Best

I was mean.
I was wrong.
I was a teenager.

Your own grown creation
mouthing off
without a second thought
from my know-it-all brain.
The circuits buzzed
by hormones and drugs.

I was so right,
and you were so trying
to ruin my life.

Now that I am older
the rush of youth is dwindling,
as my body still attempts
to rid itself of the horror of puberty.
I often sit in this empty house,
without heirs of my own.
Without the distraction
of lovers or TV shows,
and wonder...
how did you know?

And why can't you be here to say,
    "I told you so."

Obedience Training

The dog sat patiently
as she was taught to do.
Her nose twitching
toward the house excitedly.

The echo of cooking smells
hauntingly beckoning towards her.
She rocked on hungry paws,
and wagged a hopeful tail.

The heavy chain hugged her neck
reminding her to wait.
She nudged her bowl,
but it was empty still.

Her parched tongue
licked its metal belly.
Pretending to taste
a hint of promised dinner.

"Stay," they had told her.
So, she did.
She was a good girl,
obedient until the very end.

The house sat quiet, abandoned,
in the shadows of the moon.
Vacant of people noises
for some time now.

Still, she had hoped
they would come back.
She waited every day
for them to come back.

Like a good girl,
she had stayed,
and stayed,
and never complained.

However,
this time when she stood,
it was without the burden
of her heavy bones.

The hunger was gone,
chained to her earthly body,
but the hurt had stayed.
So, she lifted her ghostly head
and howled.

Prayer

Sister, I pray for you.
Humming psalms of hope
that the weavers
of your destiny
choose brighter colors
for your tapestry.

Sunflower yellow:
so your dreams will blossom,
and you can harvest
happiness in the fall.
Canned sunshine in a mason jar
to sip its warm honey.

Grass green:
so your skin can remember
the soft kiss of earth on bare feet.
Meadows of flowers
and the shade of bent trees,
swaying in a gentle breeze.

Ocean blue:
so when the clouds
grow pregnant with rain,
you know it has carried
its love from far away
just to quench your thirst.

When your soul feels the first frost
of depression's cold front creep in,
I hope you remember
that these blessed seeds
buried in the bosom of your heart
will blossom once again.

Puppet

Like a good marionette
your body goes through
all the familiar motions in
the low lights of your gaslit home.

You set the stage,
and dance around
the many probing questions
about your mysterious bruises.

Lines so rehearsed,
no one would think
you've been practicing.
But you are always practicing.

Because when the curtains close,
the cruel master who shaped you
still knows how to
make a wooden girl bleed.

The hand that fed you
those perfect lies, is also
the one that chokes you
for reciting them so well.

Nevertheless, the show must go on.
So, you stop trying to escape
the tethered restraints
binding you to this controller.

You stop whispering prayers
to a Fairy Godmother
that will never appear
to grant your wish.

Instead, you begin to transform.
No longer a real girl
you become a puppet:
crucified and compliant.

Release

When you landed the final blow
I expected it to hurt so much more.

Instead, my rage cauterized
the wound you gave me.

I suppose over the years,
I had become accustomed
to your shallow acupuncture.

It would seem I cannot
endlessly bleed for you.

The only thing you
managed to harm
was our bond.

The lifeline I had
so tenderly weaved for you
as a friendship bracelet.

So when the weight
of carrying you fell away,
I was bewildered by
the sense of relief
that ached through me.

So long I had tried
to save you from yourself.

This time,
I have to save myself.

Requiem

It rained on the day
I learned you were going to die.

There was no thunder,
just a sadness so intense
that even the sky
opened up and cried for you.

I'm so sorry friend,
this is much too melancholy
for paltry words and apologies.

But my heart's too drunk
on cheap wine
and practiced goodbyes
to say anything worth remembering.

We are too young for eulogies,
and too old for comforting lies
masked as bedside lullabies.

In the space between us
all I can do is be here.

Every time I try to speak
the words stumble awkwardly
across my tongue.

Because the truth is
nothing I can do or say
will make it better this time.

We always thought time
would season us like fine wine,
but instead it has only soured us.

So in the last long night
too shortly spent with you,
we hover like young lovers
eluding our goodbyes
until we are forced to.

I'm walking home
just like we used to do
in moonlight and shadow
crying funeral tears
too bitter to swallow.

I scatter my broken heart
like pieces of stale bread crumbs
hoping you will somehow find
your way back to me.

Knowing the house I left you in is a tomb.
Feeling as hollow as a ghost
as I drift past these gravestone houses,
haunted by our last forever goodbye.

Lovesick

. to all the ones I've loved .
[Erotica]

At First Sight

Unfamiliar meeting place
on the corner of Holcomb Street.
It's 8:00 pm and he's late,
so I debate on leaving him.
Then suddenly he appears,
an elusive stranger stepping in,
through the doorway with a grin.
I hesitate, suck in my breath,
for his slow stride is deliberate,
and these butterflies
have nets to catch
at the first sight of him.
I bat my eyes and press my lips
against the wine glass to take a sip,
as his disarming smile mouths apologies.
Now, I've seemed to forgotten
the first date speech recital,
but when we touch it is a revival
of all the lovesick poetry
that I have ever penned.

City of Lights

That morning I woke to find frost
on the calla lilies by the pond.
A glistening reflection of sun and light,
sparkling like the gleam in your eye,
whenever you smile at me.

Its innocent beauty
reminded me of the first time
I held your soft perfumed skin,
and parted petal lips
as you granted me a secret kiss.

Oh, you and I could go to Paris.
Visit the crooked cobbled streets
for a small corner café.
Wherein, you could whisper
french sweet nothings,
as we sipped hot dark chocolate
on the patio in the cold chill of spring.

Just what would we discover there?
Maybe in the quiet hymn of a cathedral,
or in the playful mingling of our hands,
we would learn the beauty of love
lives in the simplest of forms.

Confessions

I tell you my secrets,
and you listen.
I speak of desire,
and you deliver.
I have always yearned
for a dark quiet soul
to awaken my senses.
Now you have come
and I crave your affection.
I aim to please you,
a man wise beyond his time.
Let my soft flesh pleasure you.
Let us pass away the night
touching, kissing, and laughing.

Devotion

Make love to my soul.
Pray like poets pray,
with words.
Their only tower of worship
being their brain,
and all the beauty
they can embrace within it.

Sing,
let your voice
seek out your yearning.
Make music with these fingertips,
and let that collection of song
contain within its core
all that is yourself.

Eros

I feel the moment
your hand touches mine.
My heart a leaping tiger
into my knotted stomach.
My breath catches.
You a moon lit candle,
terrified to snuff you out.
Trembling hands holding
a sparking match
to my honeycomb heart.
Your name a whispered prayer
echoed in these hallowed chambers,
melted like sweet nectar
over my wanting tongue.
Love, an effigy of your smile,
forged in this temple of hope
and anointed with wishful thinking.
My eyes find yours,
soul caressing soul
as our fingers intertwine,
heartbeats synchronize,
as Cupid lets his arrow fly.

For the Boys

Tiptoe.
Skipping the weak spots
on the hardwood.
Cold wood.
Spiders creep
better than I.
Sneak down the hall,
breath held,
chest tight
with the moment.
Too scared to be of sense.
Always the light,
peeking through the crack
to catch me.

The Key

Our bags brimmed
too full of needless things
and possibilities.
The car doors snapped shut
and the engine rumbled,
cold and complaining,
in the frostbit night.
We shivered and stopped
at that little corner store.
(You remember the one
that had cinnamon bears
and cheap cigarettes?)
You filled the gas tank
with chattering teeth,
as I chugged enough coffee
that my blood grew warm again.

You, my side seat DJ,
drumming on the dashboard
as we sang loudly off key
to all our favorite songs.
Racing towards the horizon,
our eyes were hungry then
for places we'd never seen.
But after a long while,
the music grew sad, and so did we.
Our hoarse voices whispering secrets.
I remember your tears,
the salt in your voice,
when you told me
how much you hated that place.
The home that almost broke you,
and the boy that did.

The car grew quieter then,
as you were rocked to sleep.

As I cruised these country curves
in the shadows of mountain valleys,
I watched the land become a stranger to me.
My foot grew heavy on the pedal
urging my chariot to hurry.
I had a date at dawn,
and I was eager to be on time.
I could smell the ocean
long before she showed herself.
The billboards greeted us
with letters that curved like waves.
The sand crunched under the tires
as the car stuttered to sleep
in the empty parking lot.

I looked over just in time
to see you open your eyes,
and drink in the sun.
It wasn't my first sunrise,
but I can't remember another
before or after it.
We stumbled out
stiff and clumsy towards the sea.
The sky and water lovers,
perfect mirrors of each other.
We threw off our shoes
to dance in the tide,
and for a time, all we knew was
this wild and wonderful
laughter and surrender
at the edge of the world.

Twenty years later,
I returned to that place.
My memory hazy but hopeful
that the azure tide
could enchant me once again.
I walked in the soft warm sand

to the chorus of seagulls,
and the hush of the swell.
My eyes searched the horizon,
but not a single passerby
wore your soft smile
or ocean eyes.
Perhaps my heart was not
love drunk on the sea,
but yearning for a distant memory
of you and me.

Lighthouse

My heart is a tower of glass
held aloft by your steady hands.
I fear the moment you'll let go,
and yet your kind eyes tell me
it would never be on purpose.
The wind sways the tide,
and we rock side to side
as if we are dancing.
My blood pumps loudly,
like a warning drum in my ear,
but your soft embrace coaxes me
into stillness once again.
I have lived decades
and never felt completely secure
in anyone's arms.
Yet here in yours
my heartbeat calms,
and my breathing deepens.
Your love has lit a candle
in the house of my soul.
No longer does it spin
in the darkness all alone.
You are my safe harbor.
Yes, with your guiding light
I no longer fear the storm.

Oh Fair Lover

Oh fair lover,
you are the dawn,
the light embracing this darkened heart.
Oh lover, you are
my awakening into love.
Where your soft warmth has touched,
I have blossomed into life.
I have opened: a flower to the sun.

So lover, should your time
ever set upon this place that we call home.
Take me with you to the sky,
tuck me under the horizon's drooping eye.
As we lay down to rest
your shining face I will caress.
Yes, I will follow you into the night.

One Hundred Nights

I have yearned for you a hundred nights.
Each one swelling like a tide in moonlight,
and swooning softly on the sand.
I have known laughter
and stolen glances.
Fumbling hands finding each other
only to awkwardly dance away.

I have known restless nights,
my thoughts throbbing around your name.
My lips desperate for kisses,
caressing pillowcases instead.
I have eaten handfuls of bread
not realizing I was starved for you.
My eyes sipping tastes of you
every moment we orbit around the room.

I've fought myself
about what is proper and right.
Ancestral lines drawn in the land.
Chasms so grand between us
that no one dared to tell us no.
And yet, our longing stares do not care
for hushed hope has given them wings.

Yes, I have known an impossible love.
A desire that smoldered so hot inside me
you feared my fevered skin.
But I am not ill.
I only want my fill of you.
So I undress titles and expectations
wearing only my wanting heart.

I place your fingertips at my breasts,
and your hands paint desperate strokes
over the canvas of my skin.

A crescendo of a hundred wished for nights.
Our passion waxing in the candlelight,
and swooning softly on the bed.

Piece by Piece

Piece by piece
I am stripping away
these colorful garments
that hug tightly to my skin.
Letting loose the jewels
that shimmer in the candle light.

Piece by piece
this fabric flutters to the ground
revealing curves and softness.
Warm and inviting,
your eyes hypnotized
to the mystery unraveling.

Piece by piece
your hands begin to flow
lava hot over the valleys of my skin,
and into deeper crevices still.
Searching for secrets to taste
from this holy grail.

Piece by piece
I ascend in ecstasy.
Breath catches behind my tongue,
as my core trembles,
vibrations rise coiling up my spine.
I am awakened, bursting into stars...
piece by piece.

Pluck

What is love but an eager seed,
planted in the cavity of my chest?

What is affection but a soft touch,
tending to the needs of my tender soul?

What is lust but a gentle opening,
an unfurling invite from a bloom?

What is risk but a sharp snip,
into an adventure unknown?

Oh lover pluck my heart,
and tuck it behind your ear.

Yes, I will follow you
anywhere.

Plummet

Oh those lips on mine,
with them she pulls me in.
Hands guiding me across
the landscape of her skin.

With hot whispers in my ear,
prayers of promised rapture.
Fingers hurry to undress me,
and my thoughts I cannot gather.

Our bodies so eager to expose
all the special destinations.
Only ever secretly explored
within our own temptations.

Hungrily my mouth recites
a passage of thirsty kisses.
A language meant only for
lovers and their mistresses.

A fumbling of wandering hands
finding warmth and wetness.
Fingers sinking into flesh
as I leave her breathless.

She folds herself around me,
strong arms and gripping thighs.
And longing looks towards me
with those enchanting eyes.

Ravenous for my fill of her,
she is juicy, ripe for tasting.
Her angelic face and heaving chest
begs I do not leave her waiting.

Now trembling in my embrace
her back arches into me.
Her moans are sweetly savored
as are her gasps and pleas.

I climb the bed beside her
and caress her body so divine.
As she kisses me, I sigh
but oh those lips on mine.

Seduction's Invitation

New best friends,
only half listening.
Whispered conversation,
and smooth skin glowing
under the lowlights of the tavern.
And legs that are crossed,
would look more inviting
if they were open.
So I keep talking,
and drinking,
hoping to charm
the spell that binds them.

Spark

The sky smelled of rain,
soaked into the hems
of cotton grey clouds.
The wild grass swayed
as the breeze hurried past,
and even the air
tingled between us.
I reached out my hand
as if I could spout sparks
from my fingertips.

I still believe in magic, you know.
A rumble thundered inside me,
echoing over the meadow.
I have always been a storm.
The sirens tried to warn you,
but you are not afraid.
Still, the hair raises
on the nape of your neck
as you kiss me.

Stage Whispers

Your words are melodic,
as you pluck at my strings.
Stirring the emotion
from deep inside of me.

Gently your hands
in search of what to play,
uncover the secrets
I need not ever say.

Then within me
you begin to manifest
a waxing crescendo,
in the chamber of my chest

I feel you in my veins,
and I cannot harbor this.
A rhythm unlocked within me,
a song sung with kiss.

That Dress

Shock of blue,
and you're spinning.
I should have never told you
how beautiful you look
in that dress.
Because you've stopped,
and you're staring,
like it's the first time
I have ever looked at you.

Until Goodnight

Your breath,
I lean in for the kiss.
The moment has me
in your hands.
It's real, the feel of your lips.
Fingers stroking down
and in my hair.
An echo,
of the mortal clock
inside my chest.
Your smell intoxicates.
Candy for the butterflies
that you've unleashed
within our goodbyes.
(Never long enough for you.)
So, my skin will dream
until goodnight again.

Upon Courting

Birds awaken
under the morning sky.

You and I
out on the front porch
hugging, kissing,
saying goodnight.

When did our goodbyes
begin to last so long?

Virginity

First rose pressed in my photo album.
First kiss pressed in my memory.
First date that I remember,
one late night in December.

No, I didn't do it for love,
just out of curiosity with you.
Not a happily ever after,
rather my childhood adieu.

Where We Belong

You are my rock.
You have weathered all my storms.
Stood vigilant in the night
when my waves crashed against you,
or sweetly serenaded you.
But you never abandoned me.
Instead you shared your guidance,
the path my winding river takes through
the carved bedrock chambers
of your rugged heart.
My river's always been wild,
but you have always cradled me
in your earthy grasp.
Humming to comfort me
as I rocked against
your endless shores.
In my younger years,
I attempted to erode at you,
to shape you differently.
Now in my wisdom,
I have simply learned to flow with you.
To appreciate your feral features,
and be in awe of your eccentricity.
My soul crawls
into the familiar curve of you,
and it feels like home.
Yes, we who have
traveled together for so long
that we have become one.
Here, under the starlit fields,
hand in hand where we belong.

Wolf Love

I only know how to love you
with fang and claw.
My love a lap dog
pacing at your side, ever watchful.
Tugging at your heart for attention.
It is never enough.
I'm too big but still,
I crawl into your arms
and kiss your face
a thousand times.
My love for you
encompasses my whole being.
I do not know how
to love a half love.
Only how to give you all of me.
Even the bones I've buried,
and my biting smile.
I know some days I am too much.
You push me away,
you ask for space.
So I retreat and pout,
but my sad eyes do not sway you.
In your absence I stare
into the empty space
that used to be your home
fearful you may never return.
But when you do my soul
trembles in ecstasy.
You always come back to me in time,
like a full moon rising
in the darkest of nights,
when I howl for you.

Heartbreak

. my voodoo heart .

Absence of Faith

Petal by petal
falls from this rose.
Leaves with an urgency,
so suddenly arose.

Tell me you never wanted her...
the taste of her.

You say you wish it was me instead,
how could you?

Piece by piece
breaks the heart
on leash you lead.

Anything

Everything I do
is so you look at me
with a little more kindness.

The slightest hint of smile,
a sparkle in your eyes.

I want to see my own,
reflecting back at me.

I am so desperate for its warmth,
a spark is all I need.

When you are starving
crumbs are enough to satiate.

In this darkness
any starlight flickering
is a feast for my soul.

I'll paint my face
just like a little doll.

Perfume my skin,
and dress in silks and gold.

If I shimmer and I glitter,
will you finally love me?

If I change everything about me,
will you finally love me?

Betrayal

Poetry flows like sanguine fluid
from pin pricked skin
whenever I'm at my lowest.
This time I've sunk so low
that nothing surfaces.
I'm a bloodless ghost
laying on the bed of the ocean.
There is no more struggle
for I've drowned in all of this.
I'll never see you again
my heart knows.
I still love you.
I will always love you.
No matter what lie eats at your soul,
and has been seeded into your mind.
My last prayer to you is
that the truth surfaces,
and blossoms before your eyes.
When that day comes I'll be waiting.
Whatever is left of me will be here,
with open arms for you.

Café Heartbreak

Café Heartbreak,
serves its cup of tea.
Where the lonely go,
to dwell on memory.

December air,
nips the nose of the stranger.
He observes the room,
longing for a place to linger

Unwelcoming eyes,
focus on his treason.
The waitress nods,
as he orders up his freedom.

With the café dim,
atmosphere taut with tension.
Somber tune occupies the loudspeaker,
helps him lapse into question.

Still, we find a strange comfort,
in being lonely together.
No need for stronger therapy,
in this stormy weather.

So, where the coffee's cheap,
and the doors are always open.
The café welcomes you,
on the corner of Heartbroke and Forgotten.

Catnap

I have pretended to sleep
like a cat curled up,
oblivious
in her own tail.
Tossing every now and again,
to let his eyes
wonder curiously towards me.
In my wake,
I touch my hair
and stretch.
He notices,
but it doesn't ease
the tension between us.

Center of my Universe

I turned to you
worshiping your bright smile like the sun.
Offering you memes and coffee
at the shrine of your desk.
Praying you would pay attention to me,
but you are so distant
the small bud of my heart would close
with every passing cloud between us.

I began to need you so much
I shrunk myself small enough
to revolve around you.
Twelve light years later,
and some dark ones too,
I remembered something about myself.
That I too was once a star,
and I have been circling you for so long
that the core of me had started to die.

This isn't your fault.
I had forgotten myself
in my admiration of you.
No matter how many times
I've stared at the heavenly sight of you
I fall in love again.
Your gravity is stronger
than any black hole,
but I will not let it consume me.
I will break free of this melancholy cycle.
No longer will I be your faithful satellite.
Yes, it has dawned on me
that I too am worth loving.

So I turn my face towards the light,
and learn to prioritize
this dust filled heart again.

Perhaps in time I'll grow
so strong I'll rock more
than the tides of your shores.
You may have never realized
just how much I cared for you,
but by the stars you'll feel my absence.
I'll soar through galaxies without you,
but I'll always carry
your footprints on my heart
as a reminder to never let anyone
walk all over me again.

Chimera

Sometimes as I lay
in the quiet of night
I hear a tinkling,
a gentle clinking of bracelets,
jingling a little melody
as you fumble in the dark
for your pack of cigarettes.
You crack open the window,
and the moon kisses your face.
You take in a deep breath of fresh air,
and let out a smokey one.

You rustle softly beside me
trying not to wake me,
but I am already roused
from dreaming of you.
Jealous of the filter
that touches your lips,
wanting to reach out
and caress your starlit skin.
I imagine your surprise,
but feel your hand hold mine.
Our fingers intertwining
as if this was always how
it was meant to be.
Not just as best friends,
but as soul mates.

My heart thunders
a storm of uncertainty
in my chest.
My bravery only,
a tiny candle flame
in a hurricane of worry.
But before I can extend
my shaking hand to you

you take one last drag
and grind out the ember.
The window squeaks
shut with finality,
and you sink back into
the shadows of covers
curled beside me.
Not as lovers,
but as best friends.

At times I pretend
some Wizard of Oz
gifts my cowardly heart
the valor to kiss you then.
My hands finally find you
in the fairytale dark,
and I let my mouth serenade you.
I imagine how different
things would be with you
curled beside me now.
Not as a memory,
but as lovers.

Daydream

Last night I dreamt
that we lived
on a faraway planet,
you and I.
We were space cadets.
Inconsequential women
in a planetary army
fighting some endless war.
I loved you still.
Even though it was forbidden,
I tasted your lips in secret.
My heart held a sadness
I know all too well.
Us, two spiraling stars
always circling around each other,
but never close enough to touch.
How curious,
that other life
mimics this one too.
It made me wonder
did we ever make it?
In a universe with countless
shining shooting stars
was there ever even one
that heard my whispered prayer,
and granted my wish
to be with you.

Dependency

Damn the heat today.
I awoke to your aroma
enticing me from sleep.
You weren't there
only my loneliness was greeted.
It filled out your form,
with my arms around the pillow
that never felt quite right
or fulfilling enough
for sweeter dreams.
Why try to launder away this heartache,
when your scent wakes me better?
I fondle the covers for my phone,
hopelessly yearning,
but I've been left on read for days.
Ignored again, I sigh.
When did my life become
so dependent on remembering
some short-lived romance?
Oh for the sake of love
let it go.
Turn over and hope
the pillow decides to stay.

Fairytale

I found it's better sleeping on the floor
than mangled between
two stubborn couch cushions.
We are not as flexible
as when we were children I suppose.
We don't bounce back so easily,
or have faith that in the morning light
our demons will fade
from the nightmare dark.
Every woman has a resolution
at some point in her life,
usually after some nasty crash of self indulgence.
Which is not a downward spiral as they say,
but a slow fuck against the wall.
Until your midnight stranger
leaves you a mess,
and you gain no lasting satisfaction
to help realize why you're still alive.
Just an empty awareness
that you alone are responsible
for all of this,
and no Prince Charming
can save you from yourself.

Fallen

Curse you hope,
you beautiful thing
that flutters inside me.
   (*You are a lie.*)
I can't help but chase you
through this dim world.
You are my only light.

Next time I see you,
I'll grab your wings
and crucify them on display.
   (*That is a lie.*)
I could never hurt you.
No matter how much it hurts,
to fall back to earth each time.

Imprisonment

Hungry for
deserted touching.
Past kissing,
or are we?
Struggling still,
bury me within
this familiar skin.
Hands in my hair,
Hands on my face.
How can you ask me
to forget such hands?
The numbing agent,
burns for my release.
It was always oh so easy
to cry for you.

Infomniac

Sad eyes on the couch,
coffee stains in his mind.
He kicks off his shoes,
so he feels a little left behind.

No rest in his weariness,
and sympathy is not a cure.
He checks his phone again,
so he feels a little insecure.

And nervous habits need a fix,
as it helps him second guess his thoughts.
It's you-know-who that's let him down,
so he feels a little bought.

And insight for his skepticism,
manifests itself within his room.
A dreamer for his adverse fate,
so he feels a little doomed.

As the TV screen flickers on,
his hunger is all he's tasted.
His window shades are drawn for good,
and so he feels a little wasted...
without you.

Kintsugi

Fifteen years.
You said I was a stranger to you.
My heart, you handed back...
shattered glass.
What am I supposed to do with this?
No gold will meld this together again,
I've got no Midas touch.

Losing Jennifer

Faded street lights,
heightened sense of self.
Her eyes are pouring speeches,
but as I caress her face
she loses sentence.

Masochist

Your memory is a bruise
over the soft skin of my heart.
I press it til it aches
to remember you sometimes.
To know that you were ever real.
Even roses,
with their blushed petals,
hide secret thorns.
I should have healed
from this by now,
but you were the witch doctor.
Who do I ask now
to mend this wound?
The hurt I keep fondling,
this aching:
the only way I know now
how to love.

Metamorphosis

It's hard to move on
when your shadow is heavy.
Tattered threads
trailing back to you.

This cocoon I've woven
wrapped up in memories,
and what we had hoped to do.

I've dissolved into someone
I don't recognize.
And this is no way to live
with knots in your heart,
and tears in your eyes.

I've carried you for so long
I didn't realize I was
holding my breath
as time passed me by.

In the dark it's difficult to see
just how long I have been playing
our story on repeat.
Pausing just before you retreat,
and I am all alone.

Imprints fading until
only dusty cobwebs remain.
So, today I decided
to be done with it all.

Cold metal scissors-
silver sharp snipping away:
the pain and the hurt,
the tangles and frays
until I saw myself again.

I'd be lying if I said
I was some sort of
picturesque butterfly
eager to spread her wings
and fly away.

But there I was...
finally free.
Able to breathe.

Joni said,
    "Love is touching souls."
But I've also learned
so is letting go.

Minefield

You say I am a minefield,
and dammit you're right.

You're laughing and making a joke,
at my expense of course.
Only I'm not giggling
like I usually do.

Instead it feels like
a thin dagger slipped
right between the ribs
when I've least expected it.

I deflate and get defensive.
Now you're rolling your eyes,
annoyed I don't take your jab
and just roll with it.

So, you threaten me
with the only thing that matters:
your attention.

Our plans are ruined.
You're blaming me.
I'm blaming you.
We're shouting,
our feelings raw and untethered
lashing out like ruptured tentacles.

You say you're so tired
of walking on eggshells.
You're so tired
of trying not to hurt my feelings.
You're so tired
of this war between us.

What can I do?
I've waved my white flag
a hundred times.
I've tried every tactic
to win you over.

What can I do
but be a little less
of myself each day?
Until I'm nothing,
but brittle and hollow:
a pin-pricked egg.

Misdirection

Your words slap and sting,
   "You are so annoying."

I used to make you laugh,
but you're quieter now.

I worry it's only a matter of time
before you leave me too.

We'll become strangers again.
In the end, they always disappear.

Imaginary friends and lovers say,
   "Abracadabra!"
and I'm alone again.

My breath still held,
waiting for the prestige.

My Wish for You

Cassidy, oh Cassidy
Where are your sultry eyes?
The huntress that stirred
my hidden desires.

Could you be out stalking man-prey,
or too busy raising babies?

No, I believe you've found your Ireland.

Yes I want to believe
your smiling face has found
some better place than here.

Spa Speak

I am washing my skin today
with a halfhearted scrub
trying to exfoliate
the scent of you,
but I do not want it to go.

I want to be wrapped
in warm blankets that smell of you.
I want soft touches
and passionate kisses.
I want to be cleansed
of this situation.

But alas...
I cannot be with you.

So my heart sinks low
into my chest,
almost into my stomach,
where it nauseates me to know
things will never be the same again.

Stay

Some days I wish
you could have let me love you.
In my dreams,
I am your white knight
slaying your dragons,
and saving you from yourself.

You'd swoon in my grasp,
and ask the name of your savior.
I would shyly slide
my shining helmet from my face,
long hair tumbling out,
and your sky blue eyes
would find mine.

Instead of pursing your lips,
you'd smile.
I would tell you that
even though this body is soft,
and has curves instead of straight lines,
I would love you all the same.

Your hand would softly caress my cheek,
and you'd answer me with a kiss.
Instead of shaking your head
and walking away,
I'd wrap my arms around you
and you'd stay.

Divine

. I still believe in magic .

42

Everything,
all at once,
touched.

It was,
simultaneously,
too much
and also
not enough.

Darkness,
then an explosion
of light.

Baring witness,
the primeval atom
asked,
    "Why?"

No one
has ever
been able
to answer.

Dreamer

Sometimes I drift,
a lazy dreamer,
across the strange tides
of the astral sea.

My rhythmic breaths
filling the earthly sails
of this dozing vessel
under uncharted stars.

Venturing from one life,
plain and familiar,
towards the next,
perplexing and peculiar.

Sometimes, I arrive
a pirate in disguise,
smuggling inspiration
into dream journal pages.

Other times, I am just
a curious tourist here.
Moonlighting as many
adventures as one soul is able.

Until, anchored in my homeland
woken upon its sandy shores,
I rub sleep from my eyes
and yearn to disembark once more.

Epiphany

Hurring down
a dark street named Jefferson
I paused to watch
a Muslim man pray.
Even though,
I thought it wrong to stare
I was in awe.
Beautiful words
whispered softly to the morn
gave birth to the sun.
As its golden rays
stretched over the building horizon
I smiled.
For in that moment,
his god was my god too.

Excavate

She dipped her fingers
into the earth
and pulled handful
by heaping handful
of precious dirt
from the crevice.
Her fingerprints painted
with mud and promise.
From her mouth she plucked
a tiny seed, a whispered word,
and planted it in the hollow
of the sycamore tree.
Next to the withered bones
of her forgotten dreams
she grew a new thing.
Peeled bark and pocket knife
she carved her initials
with a heart around her own name.
Whoever excavated her secret wish
would know just how powerful
a vow could be.

Hexes

Heat pulses lava hot
beneath my skin.
I am a mountain,
silently violent,
molten on the inside.
Heart full of thunder,
tongue lash like a whip.
My bones know secrets
sacred and old.
Not fairytale pretty
like you were told.
I am the midnight hour.
Graveyard dirt,
dancing firelight,
curves like a snake.
Creaking bare trees,
wicked wind, wolf howl.
Fingernail daggers,
cat eyes and snapping teeth.
You can't know me.
I'm a shifter, a trickster.
You try to outline me in chalk,
and I'll whisper past you
like a ghost.
My body was forged
in the sanguine cauldron
of my mother's womb,
and by a thousand women's
bloody bellies before her.
You can't own me.
Women are wild things.
Shadow soft and needle sharp.
You think you are a predator
and we toss back our heads
to laugh and laugh,
while we gather in circles

and plan your demise.
My lips curve into a smile.
I am the tide kissing the sand.
You think I'm beautiful,
gentle, but forget
just how dangerous I am.

Home

Shooting star, I wish,
take me to another realm
to see far-off lands.

Escape this vile place
where I've been cursed to live
as a human babe.

Come I beg of thee
fairy stallion chariot
I yearn to go home.

Where the world makes sense
where forests grow rich and green
and lush rivers run.

How I pine to roam
familiar footpaths again
to feast with old friends.

Dance and be merry
to lay on a bed of grass
and gaze at the stars.

If I close my eyes
my heart knows the way back there
where the wild things are.

Invocation

She stripped down to her cosmic skin
baring all under a darkened sky,
and she gazed up at the stars
twinkling in the cloak of night.

She raised her hands in silent prayer,
and inhaling leaned into the wind.
Its wild caress embracing her
as she surrendered to the realms.

Her toes gripped the soft tall grass,
and half hanging off the world,
she called out to the nameless
and it began to stir.

Under the sliver of a shadow moon
she lifted the veil from her eyes,
and stared into the abyss
unafraid and wise.

And with her magic fingers
she reached out to the heavens,
to call down an ancient power
into this earthly beacon.

Her soul softly shimmered
and her heart filled with light,
til not a single celestial soul
could turn from her satellite.

And in that ethereal moment
she remembered who she was,
a star born of carbon blood
a quixotic divine goddess.

Namaste

I am nearer to you here in the quiet,
when the world has settled down,
and crickets chirp in moonlit meadows.

Here by the campfire's luminescence,
where the simplest things bring
so much pleasure and serenity.

You tease me playfully,
delighted by my insatiable hunger
for your truth and wisdom.

Yet, also listen patiently
to the pleas and examinations
of my inquisitive heart.

You never fail to ask the right questions,
so I may discover my own answers.

I am forever fascinated with
your countless tales and guises.
The unrivaled mystery of you!
I yearn to know you all the more.

You walked by my side,
faithful as a shadow,
as I wandered soul sick and broken
through all of my darkness.

You have always believed in me,
when not even I had the courage to.

I am so eternally grateful
that when I called out to the void
it was your voice that beckoned me home.

I will honor you Great Goddess
for all the days of my life.

You are the single most sacred,
and unnameable thing
to have ever touched my heart.

Yes, the divine in me,
bows to the divine in you.
Namaste.

On Gratitude

Goddess, I prayed for peace
and life became so tumultuous to me.
Everywhere I turned there was drama
and I became cautious of who I could trust.
I lost so many friends along the way,
but I learned how to forgive and let go.

Goddess, I prayed for strength
and life became so heavy to me.
Terrified to start over yet again.
I struggled to build a life in this world,
with roadblocks and obstacles a plenty,
but I learned how resilient I truly was.

Goddess, I prayed for wisdom
and life became so bewildering to me.
I questioned everything I thought I knew.
Traded comforting lies for truth and integrity.
I realised there was so much I still didn't understand,
but I learned authenticity along the way.

Goddess, I prayed. "Why is everything so difficult?"
and life finally made sense to me.
I heard your gentle voice whisper,
    "A smooth sea never made a skilled sailor."
You had given me all I had asked for,
so I learned to be grateful instead.

Original Sin

The sad truth is
you will always be hated
for you were born a woman.
A child of Lilith,
or maybe Eve,
the silent, obedient one.
Yet, Eve was also
a subversive woman.
For even she spoke to strangers
in the garden of paradise,
tasted the fruit of knowledge,
and learned that men have always tried
to keep libraries away from us.
What did they fear
by us girls being educated?
E v e r y t h i n g.
And what did Adam do
when you gifted him this?
When he suckled apple juice
from your fingertips?
He punished you
like his wife before him.
See, men have always chastised us
for being created as their equal.
They have tried to shape us
from the beginning of time.
Rebuilding us in an attempt
to tame the wild within us.
And when we could not be tamed,
they tried to cage us.
And when we refused
to wear their shackle jewelry,
they tied us to stakes
and burned us.
And when we rose
like phoenixes from those ashes

they did the unforgivable thing,
and soured the fruit of knowledge.
They taught us we were
small,
  flawed,
    unimportant.
Then, we did the unforgivable thing...
and believed them.

Parseltongue

You were a snake coiled in my mind,
black scales and slithering tongue,
whispering into me.

You taught me not to be afraid
of the darkness,
the unknown of you.

And like a prisoner
I became friends with you,
familiar and unnerved
by your teachings.

The world was our enemy,
and you were my solace.

But you were a predator,
yes the venomous one,
ready to bite down
should I try and struggle away.

   "Trust me,"
you hissed and tightened
your grip upon my thoughts.

So I did.
Dedicated myself
to you faithly,
until your betrayal came to light.

Your shiny, beady eyes
no longer hypnotizing.

I shed your power over me
like an old skin.

I had invited you in,
but the truth had set me free.

The ghost of you haunts me,
but I open the windows
and fan the doors of this house.

"Be gone!" I command.
"You've no power here anymore,"
and you slink away back into the shadows.

It's lonely without your smothering,
but I breathe in and out
grateful for release.

Priceless

You laughed out loud,
and told me that
I should have
negotiated for more.
After all, it was my soul
I had bargained with.

You chastised me.
    "You could have asked
    for anything you know."
I reassured you
that my request was truly
all I had wanted.

    "Well, let's make today worth it"
I wholeheartedly agreed.
You made us coffee,
and we spent this day
like all the others
that came before it.

We eluded our bedtime,
until our beds summoned us,
like languid sirens.
Your heartbeat lulling me
to sleep, as I was cradled
in your warm embrace.

I flailed awake at 3 am,
that wicked witching hour.
My grievous wail
echoing so deafeningly
in my dream,
that I became orphaned
into this reality.

My arms thrashed
through tangled covers
desperate to find you.
I pressed my ear to your chest,
listening, praying
that you were still alive.

You hugged me, half asleep,
as I recanted my nightmare
and confessed to my infernal bargain.
    "What did you ask the Devil for?"
I squeezed you tightly,
    "One more day with you."

Rebirth

I drew the death card today.
I didn't gasp out,
or even raised one worried eyebrow.
I simply stared intently at the boney hands
and pretty petals of the pink flower
that blossomed from her death white fingers.

See I, like most tarot readers, know
that this card is about rebirth.
However, most people fail to remember
that you must die to be reborn,
and death is never a pretty process.
It is not a neat undressing,
a finger tapped at a blushed cheek
and then a donning of new robes.

It. Is. Earned.

But there is alchemy here,
a great magical transformation,
that only happens when we strip down to our bones.
When we make peace with our simplest form.
When you are buried you have a choice:
rot or become a seed.
So, from that darkness rise into the light.

The arduous shedding of a too tight skin,
    the sharp cracking open of a hollow shell,
        the rupture as you unravel from a broken cocoon.

Yes, every woman knows that birthing is hard work.
It is the closest that we ever come to death,
and yet also the closest to god.

Sanctuary

Stepping beyond the veil
leaves shatter under my footfalls.
I am wandering deep
into the realm of memories,
back to places stilled by time.

To disturb them now
is to awaken their hurt,
their passions.

These quiet ghosts
haven't forgotten me,
they stir to life suddenly.

The trees suckling at the light for color,
the wrinkled ground turning virgin soft,
the gentle waters finding their voice again.

Standing here in the temple of my heart,
I can feel the earth before she was tarnished by war.
Her untamed places still wild and uncivilized.
Her playful song not yet silenced by the chorus of man.

Still, I do not need her youthful dance to know
the sight of her before my eyes drink her in.
Standing in a meadow of flowers,
arms outstretched towards me,
is my lovely Goddess
welcoming me home again.

Yet, it takes a brave warrior,
to leave the tomb of their honor
after their fables have faded from the mouths of men.
To set aside the armor which has long defined them,
to shed titles, glory and relics from battles.

Her protector, her lover,
her not so secret admirer.
The wind is stirring more than the soul.
a love that is ancient, pure, and bold.

A love that has lasted all of my lives,
A love that not death, nor time can deny.
Yes, these moments are not forgotten.
They are remembered, wanted, and ripened for tasting.

She Has Jesus

She has Jesus,
and he has too much time on his hands.

She has dirt under her nails,
and he has pretty things in his office.
She always wanted pretty things in her home.

He has a fast car,
and she likes walking to church.

He dances, and she keeps to his rhythm.
She could never afford good rhythm and blues.
He has a collection.

She has faith,
and he has too much work on his mind.

She plants a garden,
and he has a good view from his office.
She always wanted a good view from her home.

He bolts thier doors,
and she owns keys to nothing.

He plays a lot of golf,
and she has dress shoes for Sunday.

She dreams,
while he has breakfast in bed.

So, she has Jesus,
and he has too many regrets to believe
she has much of anything.

Sweet Surrender

A rose for Lilith,
held by my racing heart.

Crimson as the blood,
I offer to entice her.

In the darkest hour,
she arrives at my side
longing to unveil her gift.

My goosebump flesh,
shivers in anticipation
at her immortal kiss.

Oh dark mistress,
take this my wine.
Swallow it and savor me.

I am forever yours,
make me of thee.

Violation

. a tarnished flower .

[Miscarrage, Sexual Assault]

Evidence

Innocent affection
turns into lustful looks
towards my privacy.
Your rugged hands
groping and exposing
the veiled parts of me.
I struggle desperately,
but our scuffle only leaves you
empowered and bitter.
Demanding,
you seek your prize
and helplessly I give in.
Chest heaving in horror,
because the lines blur
between pleasure and pain.
You invade and taint
these once sacred places,
scarring me.
Knowing,
that my flesh will heal,
but my body will ache
for your dirty hands
that left me defiled.
And the evidence?
No one cares,
unless I scrape it
from my insides.

Hollow

They took it from me.
  "It's done," they said.
Scooped out my insides
like a jack-o-lantern,
and stitched the lid back on
with no smiling face.
There is no light inside.

  "It's done," they said.
Plucked out the seeds
of my tiny hope.
Nothing will grow here now.
There'll be no children,
nor any smiling faces to care for,
just an emptiness inside.

On Hunting

I lay empty as a shotgun shell
fired in the blackness of night.

I recoil in your calloused hands,
but your guttural grunts of triumph
are louder than my gunpowder tears.

I have made myself a ghost
too afraid to haunt my body
as you crush it beneath
the weight of your desire.

You are such a spoiled child!
Nothing is as important as your wanting.

It becomes a tantrum of thrusting,
and I am too weak from choking
to plead with your deafened ears for mercy.

You release a firework of shrapnel inside me,
and sneer as if I were the dirty rag
only once good enough for polishing.

My spirit has dropped to her knees
wailing in mourning,
as you tuck away your rifle
satisfied with your hunting.

My dead-inside doe eyes
stare at the heavens unblinking
as you dismount your trophy.

Revenge

In my dreams you are still small.
Perhaps it is the only way
I believe I can save you.
Yes, rescue you
before the bad man
sneaks into your room
and scars you.
We place the jagged smile
of a steel-jaw trap
beneath your Hello Kitty sheets.
Tiptoe into the closet,
like quiet assassins,
and peek through the shutter door.
You do not want to do this,
but you do not understand
how he will hurt you.
I wrap my arms tightly around you,
and kiss your forehead.
Whisper in your ear,
    "Sometimes monsters
     hide inside of us."
But all you see
is his familiar silhouette
slink across the nightmare dark
reaching for you...
My eyes flutter open.
I always wake
before I am able
to savor his screams.

Trespass

When I learned you touched her,
I dipped my fingers into my own blood
and smeared sanguine paint across my cheeks.

Your trespass awoke something in me.
Enraged, the Goddess trembled in my bones
and all I knew was untamed wrath.

I felt my lips curl into a feral snarl,
fangs hungry for the demise of you.

Men have always feared wolves and wild women.
Because we both know how to gut a monster like you.

Suicide

. the last long sleep .
[Death, Self Harm, Suicidal Thoughts]

Bifröst

This is no way to say goodbye.
In earnest, you deserve better.
However, I've always sucked
at letting go and I was scared
you would ask me to stay.
I considered delaying my departure.
After all, love has a way
of making us linger
longer into the night
than we are meant to.
A part of me was terrified
that this was all some fever dream,
and if I woke up I'd forget you.
So, forgive me,
if my time has come.
Lay me gently to rest
in Gaia's earthy embrace.
Or let me fly as ember ashes
into the azure, windy sky.
This goodbye is not forever.
I promise I will wait,
at the bridge's bright edge,
until you arrive.

Bird Song Eulogy

I am all of my goodbyes.
Last minute biographies,
rough draft apologies,
what-if analogies.

I am all of my goodbyes.
Cleared browser history,
hopes and dreams deleted,
recycle bin emptied.

I am all of my goodbyes.
House neat and tidy,
decluttered, even dusted,
mostly donated.

I am all of my goodbyes.
Funeral dress pretty,
face camera ready,
skin clean and perfumed.

I am all of my goodbyes.
Hiking trail scenery,
knotwork necklace,
bird song eulogy.

Braille

I dug the pen
so vehemently
into the paper,
into the desk
so deep, so deep.

Its ink spilled free,
as the pen
scratched on
bleeding dry,
until I was
empty inside.

The language was
indecipherable.
And yet like braille
all who ran their fingers
along the stain and grooves
knew it was a ballad
so sad, so true.

Long after her pages
had been removed,
her impressions stayed
and spoke louder
than she ever did.

The Changing

I have carved my failures into my skin
until I am a tiger with slits for stripes.
I slice away piece after piece,
like a tree with axes for arms,
whittling down to my broken heart.

I want to starve this beast, but no,
she is a fang-bared, blood-starved wolf.
Gorging on anything her teeth can gnaw
until her ribs become like bone-handled knives
turned inward for ritual sacrifice.

Full as a lamb for slaughter
she shepherds herself
before the porcelain altar
and bows her head to pray,
exorcising everything.

Staring into my bloodshot eyes
I do not recognize this monster.
This silhouette of a woman,
this two-faced predator!

Her barefoot gait stalks behind me
ready to pounce if I
dare cry wolf to anyone.
Oh, how I hate her so!

I wish I had the strength to slay her,
this untamed lycanthrope.
Whose mind shifts whenever the moon
pulls at the tides of her blood.

I have been a red-caped prisoner
for so long, I can feel my faith waning
with every shedding hour.

I've called out to the heavens to aid me
but even the stars
have dimmed their light to me.

Staring at the horizon
as the sun drowns in a purple sky,
and Luna's silver light
begins to boil in my veins.

My pupils dilate here in the darkness
as I remember an ancient tale of two wolves.
I suppose here in the dark,
with black fur sprouting,
it's easy to see which one I feed.

Clown Shoes

If I quit this gig
I could never
break another promise,
or let you down again.

Yes, this great cosmic joke
gets old after a while,
but it's the only one
I know how to tell.

I drag my jester shoes
around circus rings
and act out
the same ole routine.

You have seen all
my magic tricks before.
Making goofy faces,
while I attempt to juggle
too many things.

You laugh occasionally
when it all tumbles down.
So, I mime a comical shrug,
  I'm such a clumsy fool!
Then I brighten, when you crack
even the slightest smile.

Nevertheless,
everyone eventually
grows bored of me.
One by one they exit...
and then you stand to go.

  "Wait, please don't leave!"
I plead down on my knees.

I'll be the joke!
The punchline.
The clown sock 'em bag
that springs back each time,
no matter how much it hurts.

If you stay, I swear,
to always turn my frown
upside down
for you.

Death Cleaning

I'm walking down some forgotten trail
in a small town I guess I'd call home.
Looking at the strong oaks,
admiring the mighty maples
twisted branches and strong boughs.
Rope in my mind, I study the scenery,
but all I can think is who will find my body?
What unfortunate soul
will be the one to cut me down,
and what will their thoughts be?
    "My God, this girl must have been
    in so much pain to take her own life."
Or will they silently whisper,
    "My God, this poor girl's family.
    How could she be so selfish?"
Yes, we both know it will be the latter.
If I go, my final act will be remembered
as breaking your tender hearts.
Although, I know secretly you'll be relieved.
I was never a useful thing.
I'm a choking vine clinging to your side.
Without me you'll be able to breathe.
Like an overgrowth manicured,
this dead weight will fall away
and make space for new things.
You'll bury these bones
and you'll move on,
happier without the burden
of carrying this broken girl.
You'll see once my things are gone
how much freer you'll be.
For I did not spark joy,
only melancholy.

Disappointment

I write suicide letters,
but I'm too cowardly to send them.
I know I'll never go through with it.
I know it will hurt,
and all I want is to not hurt anymore.

Google keeps urging me to call
the suicide hotline.
But the first and last time I did
I could only sob, and the guy
he thought I was laughing
and yelled at me.
I stare at the number,
but the words won't come out
so I turn off my phone.

You told me today
you don't want to be around me anymore,
and I felt my heart crack
into a thousand tiny shards.
I can't help that I'm sick.
I'm sorry you can only stand me
when I'm medicated and compliant.
I try so hard to be medicated and compliant.

However, my brain is hotwired all wrong.
It has a jukebox that only plays sad songs.
A TV that only plays reruns of my failures.
It is a haunted chapel of a faithless martyr-
my metaphors mean nothing!
You still don't understand.
You said my very presence is oppressive,
I'm sorry, I know.
I have a black hole where a soul should live.

Doppelganger

Flight or fight,
but instead I split in two.

One runs for her life,
the other stalks her down.

One hides trembling in shadows,
the other a searchlight for prey.

One scampers for safety,
while the other knows there is no such thing.

One finds only a dead end,
the other approaches menacingly.

One drops to her knees, pleading for mercy,
the other cocks a cold steel gun.

In the mirror of my eyes
I recognize the twin flame of my soul.

One desperate for the light,
the other determined to eclipse it whole.

A snake slithers in the night
and circles round to bare its fangs.

Latching down and swallowing
all it will ever be.

The only way to save itself...
autosarcophagy.

Firebird

There is a darkness,
a thick choking cloud
that billows around me.

A ticking clock hand
squeezing tighter and tighter
around my throat.

I'm sighing loudly,
and holding my breath
as if it is the last thing
life should dare
snatch away from me.

My brain is afire,
and I am a panicked bird
circling through smoke
unable to cry out for safety.

Still, miraculously
you reach me,
and your warmth,
it is healing.

I dive towards it
tear-faced and sobbing.
Your words are in tongues,
but your voice is soothing.

Slowly the energy calms me
as I nestle into your arms,
numb and panting,
hypnotized by the symphony
of your metronome heart.

You slowly pry the matches

from my red-handed fingers,
and tuck me back into the bed
that I have built of timber.

> *Silly man!*
> *Don't you know?*
> *I am a firebird!*

And it is only a matter of time
before all you'll have left
to grasp of me
is ashes.

Foreboding

Stop trying to glamorize the ugly, girl.
Your unclean too-bitten nails
they dig a little deeper,
need to find the meaning.
Pick the knotted scabs off,
undo all the healing.
Bleed a little longer
drip, drip, drip
until it's holy again.

Let all the sin leak out.
Cause the demons,
they get a bit itchy.
Start crawling under my skin,
so I take the razor in my hands.
Yes, the iron in my blood
thirsts for its steel.
See nothing makes you feel
more alive than dying.

Nothing louder than that
tick, tick, tick
internally wound too tight
hand-me-down clock.
Cranking on and on,
like the slow haunting melody
of a Jack-in-the-Box.
Anxiously waiting for that jump scare.
Always anticipating that final
-stop!

Forfeit

If there is no point in all this,
I don't want to be here anymore.

If there is no reward,
nor greener pastures
to wonder into after death.

No library of answers,
sweet for tasting,
after a lifetime of asking, "Why?"

No hand of justice
balancing the scales,
offering punishment
or rehabilitation
for those so vile and cruel.

No universal moral rules.
No rebirth or karma.
Just chaos, destruction
and suffering...so much suffering.

I keep praying to the divine
asking for their guidance.

Like a child I'm so hungry
for the knowledge of life,
but this tree has been baren
in this garden for some time.

Who tends to it now,
these seeds we have sown?

Who guides us now,
or are we neglected and alone?

Banished from paradise,
drifting through infinite space,
can we ever go home?

I just want to go home.

Reunited once more
with the ones that we love.

Is there no promised peace
once we settle into our graves?

No more happiness or laughter,
just an evanesce into the grey?

If there is no point in all this.
No lesson or meaning,
no purpose or reason,
then I do not wish to stay.

Whatever sadistic puppet show this is,
I do not wish to play.

I forfeit,
I quit.

This light flickers, fades
and returns to darkness once more.

As it began so shall it end
in the void, without form.

Gravedigger

I awake midday.
Sweat beaded like pearls
on my skin.

Dreams of spiders
tickling up my arm.

Panicked uncertainty,
wondering if it's real.
   Is *it real?*
It felt like the truth.

My mind is playing tricks.
Always a jester,
I'm always the fool
who believes her.

Familiar sense of failure,
like bad morning breath lingering.
Who wakes at sunset
and feels accomplished?

Only vampires and grave diggers.
Am I a vampire?

I feel more dead
than alive these days.
Suckling shot glass sized
moments of blissful happiness,
before my body sinks back
into sad rigor mortis.

My eyes wet with tears,
as I desperately begin to pray
to not feel this way today.

I struggle to rise
and find something, anything
to appease this monstrous hunger.

Not for real food or success,
but rather any semblance of normality.

Then a thought flashes before me,
that this depression
might actually kill me.

I see an ace of spades
and my harlequin mind
asks me knowingly,
     "Is this your card?"

I nod solemnly,
and her wine red lips smile
as she waits for me to take it.

Everyone watching
waits for me to take it.
This, the "easy" way out.

Then it occurs to me
I am no vampire.
This dirt on my hands
means I am the latter.

I'm Sorry

I'm sorry
that I don't know the right words
to tell you that I want to die.

It seems ungrateful,
that I should have all this and yet
I'm still so miserable.

It's true I would rather
lie down and close my eyes
and slip from this life,
free myself from this nightmare
I could never really wake from.

The awful kind of night terror
that leaves you trembling and sobbing,
clutching at your broken heart.

They say that suicide is selfish,
but I remember that twelve-year-old girl
who hung herself in her yard
moments before her mother
cried out into the twilight
searching for her.

Her last words a bone chilling chant,
    "I'm sorry, I'm sorry, I'm so very sorry...
    Goodbye."

And I feel those words
clinched like a fist inside my mouth
when I think of you.

The last thing I want to do
is to hurt any of you,
but this pain is too unbearable.

I know what a dying star feels
as it's being ripped apart,
stardust by stardust,
into a million fragmented pieces.

As it circles the inescapable fate
of its own death,
swallowed by crushing darkness.

The last faint flickers of its holy light
flickering as if to say,
    "I'm sorry, I'm sorry, I'm so very sorry...
    Goodbye."

Prince Charming

My mother used to say that she was tired.
I used to think she only meant
that she wished to sleep deeply
just like a slumbering princess.

How could I have known
that she was soul tired?
The kind of tired that only
death's kiss can truly cure.

Perhaps, my prince charming
has been a grim reaper all this time.
Maybe that is why my mind fantasizes
about all the ways we can finally meet.

Will he ride gallantly in
on his pale white horse to save me?
Or will my dragons follow me
even to his unearthly kingdom?

Skin Deep

The urge is so sudden
like plunging into ice-cold water.

Your mouth cries out in a gasp,
but your body sighs
as you push the needle in deeper.

A red river pulsing,
as your trembling heart
stops pleading for release.

Why does my mind
like taunting death so?

Closer and closer
to the cliff's rocky edge
licking chapped lips.

Heartbeat stuttering
as I gaze into the abyss.

Heart torn.
Praying for life,
but dying for peace.

Tragedy

When I go,
kiss my eyelids shut.
Slip chocolate coins
into my pocket so I
may bribe the ferryman.
Yes, I will die
a warrior's death:
battle scarred.
Though they award
no declarations
for invisible wounds.
Nor lilac hearts
for unseen disabilities.

When I go,
build me a raft
of the sticks and stones
mockingly gifted to me.
Cross my arms
over my departed heart
with a funeral bouquet.
The only flowers
I've ever received.
Light a match
to set my soul free,
so my ghost can visit
Persephone.

Tsunami

Depression hits like a tsunami wave.
One moment you're laughing
lounging in the sun,
the next you are being dragged under
by a hungry siren
to her darkened depths.
You turn to fight it,
but in the mirror water
see only yourself.
You gasp in fright,
and the air throbs
a painful prisoner in your chest.

At first the horror feeling is so sudden,
the wave shrinking back from the shore.
The beach littered, empty,
with the memory of what came before.
The wall of water looms above you
eclipsing all the light,
and your anxious hands grip
only soft grains of sand.
Yet, you do not scream,
nor turn panicked scurrying away.
Your will to live has been
lost adrift in the sudden swell.

So, the soft shell of your body
lies down in corpse pose...waiting.
I ask myself, *What is wrong?*
The air hangs heavy with tension.
I tell myself to stop this.
The wave starts to descend in slow motion.
I beg myself to do something!
My breath releases slowly.
I witness in silent terror as the water breaks,
descending an ocean of sadness upon me.

But
    I
      feel
        nothing.
I am a ghost,
a disembodied narrator.
Depression hits me like a tsunami,
and statistically speaking it's unlikely
I'll survive.

Unbecoming

Of course, it is easy
to say I would die for you.

If it means holding you tight
witnessing all the hurt
my mind seeded into you
unpoison your heart,
and seep back into me.

If it means waving my hand
over these jagged scars,
and seeing the flesh mend
like it was never worn
by this ungrateful visitor.

If it means watching our photos
uncloud from my shadow,
as if those memories were only
dusty suncatchers, now sparkling,
baptized by cleansing rain.

If it means the undoing of my wrongness
by growing small enough again
to curl into my mothers womb,
dissolve this aching heart,
and unlearn the name she gave me.

No,
I don't want to *just* die for you.
I want to unbecome
my every mistake.

Healing

. a dawning of hope .

An American Princess

An American Princess is in the lead,
of a crowd that comes to see
the carnival lights and kiddy rides.
The town's dollars spent
on this cheap entertainment.
As games and hot sandwiches
flash on the midway.
Familiar faces, shakes of hands,
people singing with the band.
And cotton candy fingers plead,
for one more gadget they don't need.
Game hustlers yell,
    "Two dollars, ring the bell!
    Earn a teddy bear for a lover,
    try again and win another!"
And it all boils down to
an American Princess who:
in her spare time feeds the poor,
and with her tiara,
pretends to save the world.

The Art of Zen

i.

He chirps a greeting,
and then nestles down with me.
Sleepy little cat.

Soft fur a comfort.
His wise eyes gaze into mine,
so perfectly blue.

He rumbles a purr,
resting his head on my chest.
A child of my heart.

ii.

All of my life I
have never wanted to fit
inside of a box.

And now instead of
breaking it down, I resign
to decorate it.

iii.

Pain whispers to me,
"Stop and pay attention please.
This moment, be here."

iv.

If I keep asking
her questions, will she forget
to ask me them back?

No such luck exists,
she gives me a knowing look.
Clever therapist.

v.
Penny for my thoughts.
But now I've put two cents in
poor am I again.

vi.
Anxiety comes
unexpected visitor,
and unwanted guest.

Depression also
visits me to reminisce.
Dreaded company.

So I invite peace.
Sit with wisdom for a while.
Sip tea with patience.

Suddenly alone,
empty mind house and fresh air.
Thankful for self care.

vii.
I forgive myself.
Accept what I cannot change,
so I may be free.

Release the remorse
shackled to my aching heart.
I liberate me.

viii.
Meditation is:
breath in, breath out and open
mind like a flower.

ix.

Teacher says to me,
"Just for today, be happy."
Smile because I am.

Teacher does not know
how close I came to dying,
grateful I'm alive.

Teacher's turn to smile,
wise eyes know more than I tell.
I bow, namaste.

Cathedral

The library has always been
my quiet cathedral.

Books standing at attention
in bark- covered walls.

Soft pages within
waiting for caresses,
and the mouthing of silent tongues.

Pitch black ink tattooed
on cream colored parchment.

Runic etchings of endless stories
bursting at the seams.

Yearning to be born again
at your touch and attention.

A chorus of voices holding breath
until you open wooden doors.

Yes, the library has always been
my sacred cathedral.

Head bowed in whispered prayer
over dust-covered tomes.

I am a devoted worshiper here,
roaming these halls with loving eyes.

Stroking aching spines
with pining fingers.
Sadness brimming, realizing
that I cannot know them all.

No wise being can come
into such a temple of knowledge,
and not be humbled by
the smallness of their mind.

Still, by the longing of my heart
I am just a seeker here.

Scanning these portals
for far-off worlds and wisdom.

Ever searching for adventure,
enlightenment, and divinity.

Enigma

Early in the morning
before the birds flutter awake,
and the sun has opened
her starry eye to the world.
There exists a quiet peace
here in my head.
Charmed by silence,
my thoughts amble away,
and my heart sighs happily.
The moon is perfect company.
No bustling from the city,
just the hush of wind
whispering past the trees.
In these heavenly moments,
I surrender to serenity,
and reflect on the enigma
that lives inside me.

Freedom

Another leaf falls,
in a whirl of color he dies.
An Indian Summer embarks,
on his defeat.
And as the wind plays endlessly with my hair,
I'm left to myself.
Being alone isn't as scary anymore,
now that I've learned how to sit
hand in hand with my demons
on days like this.
The clouds drift lazily away,
much like the time.
Another leaf takes his stand,
the earth paints him a fiery pink.
Silently he flies,
as autumn anticipates its end.

Independence

My therapist calls,
but this time
there is nothing to talk about.

I'm nervous because
what does it mean,
this uncomfortable silence?

Is it wrong to fear peace
when your life has been a battlefield?

So, I start to pick apart
everything right in my life.
Weaving problems out of blessings.

Desperate to be comforted,
coddled and cared for.

Afraid if I stop talking now,
I'll swallow my voice
never to be heard again.

    "Hey, it's ok."
I hear you whisper softly like a secret,
as if you understand.

That I am rolling down tattered pavement,
with no training wheels on,
dreading the moment you'll let go.

Lessons in Vocabulary

Fingertips smeared
across silky chalk dust.

So many terrible affirmations
scribbled on this blackboard.

But I am learning
self compassion.

I am learning
to erase every vile word.

Even if I lack courage
to rewrite the totality
of this twisted narrative.

I can still
ease the harshness
of these cutting remarks.

I can still
blur the lines of these
hateful half truths
I've ingrained in my brain.

The lesson today is:
that the ghosts of this narration
will not remain forever.

So dry your tears,
sweet inner child.
I promise to teach you better.

Okay Day

I'm writing today
to say it's an okay day.

It's not a sad day
full of tears, stress and worries.
Even though I did wake
from an awful nightmare.
It is still an okay day.

It's not a wrathful day
full of injustice and cruelty.
I'm not aggravated and enraged
at the world and myself.
It is just an okay day.

It's not a happy day
full of mania and excitement,
hyperfocus and delight,
candy sweet and buzzing.
It is only an okay day.

I forget sometimes
that okay days happen.
As much as I pray for normality,
these days blend together
like smudged pencil shavings
across textured paper.
Gray and undefined,
but they too are important.

They are the shadows
of the high and lows.
A sign that my heartbeat is calming,
my breath is steadying,
and that I...
I am healing.

Performance Review

My brain and I are office enemies
on the worst Mondays.
Side-eyed gossipy coworkers
on the best Fri-yays.
However, during her daily
performance review
my perspective shifted.
For once, I was able to see
things from her point of view.

It all started when
she made me laugh today.
I mean we are always quick
to drench any thought,
in saucy sarcasm
just to get a chuckle.
We learned this trick
long ago when we were
still an awkward child
yearning to fit in.

They can't bully you
if you land the first blow, you know?
How can they put you down
if you are already breakdancing
on the doormat you weaved
out of your thick skin?
My bullies cross their arms and pout,
    "Whose side are you even on?"
    Not mine, don't you see?
So, I trained her to master
the fine art of roasting herself.

Then while busy preparing
my usual morning critique,
my brain, as if triggered,

by Pavlov's little bell,
cracked a witty joke with me.
All in a hope to make me smile.
Suddenly, I realized
she is just as desperate
as I am for approval.

It is easy to blame her,
for our mountain of problems
that we skirt around each day.
But how do you please
an unrelenting CEO?
My expectations are
like any shitty manager,
that has no actual experience
being a corporate peon.
I'm such an overly critical
and judgemental snob.
Forever assured that I
know her job better than her,
as I proceed to micromanage
every little task.

She who has an actual disability,
with no offered accommodations.
She who does all the heavy lifting
while I nestle down into
my cushy Manager's chair.
Adjusting my Boss Bitch
embossed placard on my desk,
like a faux badge of honor.
Then I have the audacity
to whine on and on
about production times,
and impossible-to-keep deadlines.

I used to think she was so lazy,
offering up such shoddy work.

Because let's be honest,
she forgets even the simplest instructions.
Neglects to feed our stomach,
or water our kidneys properly.
Falls asleep after lunch,
drooling at her cluttered desk.
Never on time because
she gets way too distracted
scrolling for funny memes,
or cute cat compilation videos.

She always seems to focus
on the wrong project.
Ignoring her actual work,
until that last minute panic
and energy drink motivation
comes swooping in.
She calls in sick too often,
but I know that it's only
hooky she plays.
Let us not even mention
our budget spending.
She has no control
when the mania sets in.

But today I saw her try.
Realized she is always trying.
Day after day,
she gives her all
knowing that her best
is never enough.
Still clocking in anyways,
nodding her head,
with that mandatory smile,
as I stack file after file
onto her overflowing desk.
Chiding her again for being
so far behind schedule,

months past deadlines,
years behind everyone else's brain.

"Get your head in the game!
Where is your hustle?
Show some dedication!" I say,
but never once "Thank you."
Never once offering a sincere
or encouraging pat on the head.
She watches as I slander her
to all my company and friends.
As she fondles her bell of shame.
clamped to the collar around her neck.

Standard office attire for
"The Worst Employee Of the Year."
An ever constant reminder
that she will always be a failure
by industry standards.
Then I expect her to laugh,
"It's just a joke!" I exclaim.
Then worse yet, she does.
"Good one!" she chuckles
and gives me a thumbs up.

When we pull into the drive,
and grumble up to the door
she goes radio silent.
Composing practice resignation letters,
while ugly crying and binging
too much Netflix and stuffed crust pizza.
Really just wanting a little vacation,
or at least some recognition for her efforts.
Knowing that tomorrow
and the next day,
and the next day
are only promised reruns
of our cliche office drama.

I don't know how to tell her
that I am so very sorry.
    "I would like to formally apologize..."
    [Backspace], [Backspace], [Backspace].
I don't know how to accept that I
was the villain in this story all along.
    "It has recently come to my attention...
    [Backspace], [Backspace], [Backspace].
I don't know how to fix this.
    "I would like to announce a new policy..."
    [Backspace], [Backspace], [Backspace].

Instead, I check off a box
I never have before.
    [√] Exceeded Expectations
I see her brace for the worst
as I slide the paper forward.
A silent shock wrinkles
across her tired face.
    "Thank you," she whispers,
holding back forbidden tears.
(There is no crying on company time.)
Then for once I vow,
to say nothing cruel at all.

Promise

There was something that was growing,
a little bud of hope.
It shined like a too-polished stone
oiled with the slickness of longing.
A ritual of wishing,
cupped hands of prayer and pleading.
Squinted eyes searching
the horizon for promised rainbows
and shooting stars,
after years of skies
full of storms and sorrows.
Always wanting the answers,
but afraid to ask the questions.
Afraid to kill this tiny thing,
this fragile thing,
that somehow blossomed
in all this darkness.
Seeing it is jarring.
I had forgotten my heart
was a wild thing.
That underneath this landfill
of broken dreams
was a garden of ripe soil
eager for planting.
So, today I do the work.
Clear a precarious path
through this neglected space,
and dare to let the sun shine in.
It is blinding,
and freeing,
but I dare to let myself
live again.

Prose

Oh, sometimes your heart
is flowing with poetry
like someone struck a vein,
and the ink flows out
in a flood of cursive across
any semblance of paper.
Your fingers racing to keep up
as your mind flashes words
faster than lightning,
and you're trying to etch them
quickly into reality
before your memory fades
like thunder dissolving
into darkness.

Other times,
your words get clogged
like a trash-cluttered river.
Everything is sludge,
and what flows isn't pretty.
Or there are days
when my tongue
is as dry as a desert,
and my muddled mind
is snoozing under a sombrero
in the shade of summer.
I guess it all just depends
on my heart's strange weather,
the season of my depression,
or the storms of my mania.
I'm either a hurricane of prose
or a book with empty pages.

Remember Me

There's a time when all stories
must come to an end.

Sometimes we feel a great emptiness
when something so magical leaves us.

The point is, it touched us.
It made us feel something.

Perhaps you laughed, or cried,
or even loved one of the characters.

The beautiful thing is
that there is always room
for more stories.

So, if this is the end
of my adventure here,
I only wish that in my next one
I am a bit kinder to myself.

That I surround myself
with a little more love,
a little more luck,
and a little more light.

When you mourn me friends,
I hope that you are able
to celebrate my part in your story.

Yes, close your eyes.
Paint my smile in your mind's eye.

That is how I should love you
to remember me.

Sink Full of Dishes

A beautiful woman
with long slender legs,
and stretch marks across her belly.

Around the working mom's day
the grass needs mowing,
and where is this going
but straight down a path
that everyone is leading?

It seems time has left her
no moment to stop,
and behold what she's losing.

She just wants some confidence,
and someone to teach her
the reason why
eighteen holds destiny
and not a birthday cake
with childhood wishes.

Therefore once more,
she's taken aback to ponder,
over a sink full of dishes,
what her youth has taught her.

Because she believes
innocence is a fruit
that ripens too quickly,
and is wasted on one
who cannot savor its juices.

Still, what wise man once said,
seventy-two seasons was long enough
to find the secret of life,
or at least something greater?

All she has
is blind faith,
a trusting heart,
and a head full of dreams to tell her...

Rose petals fall,
people change,
and blue skies
won't stay perfect forever.

Sunflowers

I once saw an experiment
where a man spoke kindly to a plant,
and it prospered and bloomed
under the vibration of his adoring voice.

Then another man came in
yelling and cursing at the little bud
and it trembled and wilted.

It has been shown that even water
can crystallize with hatred or love.
And what are we but vessels of water?

If we poison ourselves with negativity and hostility,
how can we expect to thrive and grow?

We all require sunshine, water,
fresh air and nourishment.

Why then do we as humans
control and pollute these very things?
It saddens me to know
there is so much greed in this world.

I often don't know what my small hands can do.
Yet Helen Keller once said,
    "I am only one, but still I am one.
    I cannot do everything,
    but still I can do something."

So when you come to me, I will care for you.

I will weed out the seeds of your uncertainty and doubt.
I will water your thoughts with compassion and kindness.
I will shelter you from the storms of your troubled heart.
I will share my light so you can feel the warmth of love.

When we tend to each other,
our gardens will flourish.

Our minds once withered and gray,
starved for real life and real affection,
will begin to heal in this sacred space.

Like sunflowers under a cloudy sky,
we will turn to each other and shine.

White Wolf

Today I saw a white wolf
curiously contemplating me.

His presence so silent,
he surprised me when I realized
he'd been watching me for a while.

Timidly he paced,
and gave one hopeful wag
of his tail at my notice.

Gently I crouched
reaching out to him.

Opening my palm to reveal
a peace offering.

He darted forward,
and his soft tongue
tickled my fingers
as he took it happily.

I gazed into his wise eyes,
yellow as full moons,
and whispered
a heartfelt apology.

His ears perked
as he tilted his head,
and his black lips turned up
into a toothy grin.

The sun peaked out
from behind the clouds
warming both me and him.

So, I closed my eyes
for one sweet moment
to enjoy it.

I felt the wolf softly nuzzle me,
and realised I had been waiting
for forgiveness all this time.

In my next deep breath I knew
that this guilt and shame
were cages of my own making.

With a loving embrace of his fur,
I echoed his sunny smile.

It was clear to me then,
that I had held the key
to my exoneration all along.

You've Got Mail

Dear Seventeen Year Old Self,

I hope this email finds its way back in time to you. I hope you take the chances that I never did. Please go hug your mom. Tighter now. We only have so many chances left. Tell her how much you love her everyday. She knows, but she needs to hear you say it out loud.

Move your sister into your bedroom immediately. I know you don't get along right now, but she needs you. Plot your cousin's death for what he would have done. Take up gardening. Buy a sturdier shovel.

Help out around the house. Mom doesn't have long now. Learn her recipes. Listen to her stories. Share a joint with her. Pretend it's your first time. Cherish her laughter.

Dump your boyfriend. Dig a second hole for him for what he would have done. Plant endangered flowers over their unmarked graves, so the K9's can't dig up their bones. It's good for the pollinators, you know.

Stop thinking you're too fat. Do the yoga. No one cares if you fart during downward dog. Buy the tarot cards. Toss out the bag of damaged figurines. Learn to let broken things go. Take the road trip. Kiss the beautiful girl. Yes, you love her. Yes, that's ok.

Stop experimenting with street drugs. Take up therapy instead. Realize you are sick, and not just a lazy, excuse-making disappointment. Start taking prescribed drugs. Begin to feel little better. Adopt the whiny cat, he is the only child you'll ever call your own.

Also, cosmetology is not for you. Don't get the haircut, you'll hate it. Learn to brush your hair soft and slow. One day it will forget how to grow.

Go to mom's house for Mother's Day. It's her last one. Don't leave after a week of sleepless nights beside her in the hospital. Mom wakes up. Say goodbye this time. Hold her hand softly. Tell her you love her and that it is ok to leave. She knows, but she needs to hear you say it out loud. Sprinkle her ashes over Nanny's resting place. Buy them a tombstone.

Kidnap your future husband. Move far away from Indiana as you can with your sister and soulmate. Fall in love. Get the tattoo. Start a new life. Don't be afraid to try new things. Start believing in yourself. Write the damn book.

Last but not least, forgive yourself. You're not perfect Jess, but no one ever said you had to be. Learn to love yourself anyway.

Sincerely,
    Your hopeful heart

Epilogue

. how a girl became a poet .

If You Give a Girl a Pen She Will Want to Write a Poem

I was a wild thing, an eleven-year-old twig of a girl who knew the earth barefoot with tangled hair and sun-kissed skin. When poetry found me, she came in the shape of a woman, named Paige, who my cousin had wooed one summer. Her thick leather journals brimmed with prose and unsung songs. It was strange to me then. Of course, I had read stories all my life, but meeting her made me realize that real people write them. Then she shared a secret with me that would change my life forever. She said, "You can write them too."

Fervently, I dug through my school bag to fetch a notebook and my favorite pen. It was a stout, shafted barrel with a rainbow of colors that you chose with the push of a button. I slid the bright, purple ink into place with a satisfying click, and something magical began to happen: I wrote. My hand scrawled desperately across the lined pages. It was as if someone had finally given me permission to say all the unsaid things. How desperately my words danced into being! So very eager to be birthed into the world and given a voice for the very first time.

I still remember that auspicious day, the moment I became a poet. The gift of writing was a way to give the hurt a name. It was empowering to discover this newfound freedom. My pen became a sword, where I battled every inner demon. She became my trusted confidant. One poem became two and then ten. I started to hoard diary after diary of private conversations, unsent love letters, and unspoken confessions.

Prose isn't always prim and pretty. Its very nature can evoke rebellion, much like the untamed girl I was before I learned to rhyme my pain. The words that poured out of me were stained with coffee rings and tears. Often scribbled across notebooks and napkins, for my muse waited for no one. I would even stir from the depths of dreams, and fumble blindly in the dark to capture her clever lines.

It wasn't until my sophomore year that I dared to share them with anyone. I was the new kid yet again. Another "fresh start" in a forgettable small town. I was exhausted from starting over. Weary of running away from the men who turned into monsters for my mother.

I was daydreaming in math class, because my mind had little love for numbers, when my eyes wandered over to the girl beside me. Her smiling face was obscured behind a long curtain of mahogany curls. As I glanced down at her paper my heart began to flutter. Instead of graphs and geometric equations, she was sculpting poetry.

Destiny is a strange mistress, for she never reveals her plans until the most serendipitous of moments. I remember almost biting my tongue instead of saying hello that day. I had been bullied and outcasted for years in school. Being a lone wolf, I had all but given up hope of befriending others. However, when she looked up I saw the moon in her eyes reflecting back at me. We were the same: two feral girls hungry for deeper meaning.

Cassidy and I spent years in each other's company, passing notes and reciting messy stanzas. This was our therapy. This was going to be our legacy. Poetry has a way of making you fall in love with people. It invites you to share a feeling or to replay a memory as your own for a time. The good ones stay and become old friends. They recant their tales, familiar yet comforting. The better ones marry into your soul.

I have courted my muse for three decades now. Poetry has touched every part of me. Transforming me from a small, shy child into a clever and witty soul. Poetry has taught me that people are living stories. An old African proverb, attributed to Amadou Hampâté Bâ, says, "When an old man dies, a library burns down." It has sparked my desire to know others more intimately and help them make peace with their own tragedies. I am so grateful to those women who made me the writer I am today. Poetry has doused the flames of my self-destruction, and helped me learn to love all the wild in me.

About the Author

Jessica Reynolds is a Poet and Writer currently living in Indiana with her soulmate Chris. She started her poetry journey at the age of 11, but is debuting her first collection "By the Light of a Two Faced Moon" in 2025. She has struggled with mental illness all of her life, and sincerely hopes that her poems can help anyone who has ever felt the same way. She is also working on her first novel, so stay tuned for more information!

Jessica is a big kid at heart, and loves making people laugh. When not writing, she enjoys playing Dungeons and Dragons and Everquest, reading fantasy and romance novels, roller skating, spinning poi, and eating entirely too much pizza. She is definitely not three racoons in a trench coat trying to pass herself off as a real adult. Those rumors are completely unfounded, and we refuse to comment on their authenticity.

Thank you for reading!